THE TENDER TRAP

THE TENDER

Random House
New York

TRAP

A Comedy by

Max Shulman *and* Robert Paul Smith

To Without Whom

THE TENDER TRAP was first presented by Clinton Wilder at the Longacre Theatre, New York City, October 13, 1954, with the following cast:

(IN ORDER OF THEIR APPEARANCE)

CHARLIE READER	Ronny Graham
POPPY MATSON	Parker McCormick
JOE MCCALL	Robert Preston
JESSICA COLLINS	Julia Meade
SYLVIA CREWES	Kim Hunter
JULIE GILLIS	Janet Riley
EARL LINDQUIST	Jack Manning
SOL SCHWARTZ	Joey Faye

Directed by Michael Gordon

Setting and lighting by Paul Morrison

Costumes by Anna Hill Johnstone

Stage managed by Robert Downing *and* Peter Turgeon

SCENES

Time: The present.

Place: The New York apartment of Charlie Reader.

ACT ONE
Scene I. Six P.M., Saturday.
Scene II. One-thirty, P.M., the following day.

ACT TWO
Six P.M., Saturday, three weeks later.

ACT THREE
The next morning.

ACT ONE

ACT ONE

Scene I

Six P.M., Saturday.

At rise the stage is in almost total darkness, but we are able to detect the presence on the couch of a man and woman, kissing each other. These two are CHARLIE READER *and* POPPY MATSON. CHARLIE *is a pleasant-looking man in his early thirties.* POPPY *is the same age and even prettier. She is well-spoken and excellently groomed. She seems to be thoroughly enjoying what she is doing with* CHARLIE, *as her first speech indicates.*

POPPY

Mmm.

CHARLIE

Is that the best you've got to say?

POPPY

What do you want—a testimonial?

CHARLIE

Yeah, that'd be nice. Complete this sentence in twenty-five words or less: I like Charlie Reader because—

POPPY

I like Charlie Reader because he is trustworthy, loyal, thrifty, brave, and clean in mind, body and spirit.

3

CHARLIE

You forgot "reverent."

POPPY

And reverent.
> (CHARLIE *starts to give her another playful kiss, but then they really get interested. After a considerable silence,* CHARLIE *comes up for air.*)

CHARLIE

You know, I've been meaning to tell you something for months.

POPPY

Yeah?

CHARLIE

You are the *softest* girl.

POPPY

Gee, thanks. That's what every girl wants to hear.

CHARLIE

No, I mean it. You're not flabby or anything like that; just soft. . . . You know what I mean.
> (*He proceeds to show her.*)

POPPY

Oooh! . . . Yes, I get the idea. (*They laugh and go back into a clinch when the doorbell rings. They pull apart*) Who's that?

CHARLIE

Damn' if I know, but whoever it is, I don't want any.

POPPY

(Rises, indicates she ought to conceal herself)
Hadn't I better?

CHARLIE

Maybe you ought to—just for a minute.

POPPY

Don't worry—I'll be as quiet as a mouse.

CHARLIE

But don't lose the place.
(She ducks into the kitchen, closing the door behind her. CHARLIE *switches on the lights and opens the front door. In the doorway is a man with a suitcase. This is* JOE MCCALL. JOE *is the same age as* CHARLIE, *but he shows a few more signs of wear.)*

JOE

Hiya, Charlie.

CHARLIE

Joe! *(He grabs* JOE's *hand and shakes it vigorously)* Come on in, come on in! How the hell are you? How's Ethel? Damn, it's good to see you! How about a drink? *(He takes* JOE's *suitcase and ushers him in)* Why don't you tell a fellow you're coming? *(Making no attempt to reply to* CHARLIE, JOE *sinks wearily into a chair)* What are you doing in town? Business trip? Pleasure? Or what? Family all right? How's everything back in Indianapolis?

JOE

Yeah.

5

CHARLIE

Did you have a comfortable . . . yeah, what?

JOE

Yeah, I'll have a drink.

CHARLIE

Sure thing. (*He goes to the bar*) You take Scotch, don't you? . . . Hey, wait a minute. You don't drink.

JOE

I do now.

CHARLIE

Well, congratulations. Glad to have you aboard. What'll it be?

JOE

Anything.

CHARLIE

Soda or water?

JOE

Nothing.

CHARLIE

You mean you want a shot?

JOE

That's what I want.

CHARLIE

Hey, you must be in trouble. (*He hands* JOE *the drink and starts for another glass.* JOE *tosses off his shot and hands*

6

back the glass for a refill) You must be in *big* trouble. (*He pours* JOE *another. He finds* JOE *at his elbow. He hands him the drink*) And you're the guy who used to make a long evening out of a short beer. What happened to you? (JOE *downs his drink without answering*) Hey, wait a minute, Joe. Everything's all right at home, isn't it?

JOE

Sure.

CHARLIE

Nothing wrong between you and Ethel?

JOE

(*Still wandering around the room*)

No.

CHARLIE

Are the kids all right?

JOE

Fine.

CHARLIE

Then it can only be one thing: you murdered the boss.

JOE

No.

CHARLIE

Why the hell not?

JOE

No guts.

7

CHARLIE

All right, Joe, what's up?

JOE

(*Taking in the room*)
Terrace, eh? Just like in the movies.

CHARLIE

What are you doing in New York?

JOE

Well, as a matter of fact, I'm in a little bit of a jam and I need your help.

CHARLIE

You need *my* help?

JOE

Ridiculous, isn't it?

CHARLIE

This is the switch of all time. . . . Here, have another drink. . . . No, you'd better not. You'd better tell me while you can still talk.

JOE

Now, wait a minute. Let me settle down first. (*His inspection of the apartment is over. He is now looking closely at* CHARLIE) You're looking good. (*He pokes* CHARLIE's *belly*) Say—not bad.

CHARLIE

Hell, I'm just a boy.

8

JOE

You must be taking Van Husen's vitamin pills yourself.

CHARLIE

Van Husen! How is the old crock? Still the same?

JOE

He's worse.

CHARLIE

Boy, how can you stand that man?

JOE

I can't stand him—but he still knows more chemistry than any six guys in the country—or used to, anyhow.

CHARLIE

He's a smart old weasel. Don't forget—it was his idea to take me out of the lab and make me a salesman.

JOE

If he's so smart, how come he let you in the lab in the first place?

CHARLIE

Huh?

JOE

Charlie, the mind trembles—you handling all those chemicals!

CHARLIE

Aw, knock it off, Joe. For years you've been spreading the rumor about me being the clumsiest kid in Indianapolis. Well, I've been thinking it over. It's not true.

JOE

No? Name me one other kid who fell out of a treehouse six times in one summer.

CHARLIE

Four times.

JOE

Six.

CHARLIE

All right, Frank Merriwell. Everybody can't be as smart as you. You know how to do everything. Even with girls.

JOE

Hey, Charlie, you're thirty-five years old. You're not still brooding about the junior prom, are you?

CHARLIE

You're damned right I am. Three hundred creamy girls all in a row, and right at the head of the line this lovely, sweet, soft absolute doll of a girl smiling at me. All I have to do is walk three paces forward and say, "May I have the pleasure of this dance?" But all of a sudden, 'way down at the end of the line, I spot this tall job—the cuckoo one with the hot eyes. So what do I do? I cut my way through half a mile of organdie, while you take the simple three paces forward. You get Ethel—I get slapped with a paternity suit.

JOE

Well, at least they cleared you.

CHARLIE

Why shouldn't they? I never even laid a glove on her.

JOE

You know, that's what Ethel said. From the beginning, she said, "Charlie couldn't have done it. . . ."

CHARLIE

You're damned right.

JOE
(*Continues*)
"He hasn't got the know-how." Poor Charlie! You never had any luck with girls, did you?

CHARLIE

No, but you did. How is she?

JOE

Ethel? Fine.

CHARLIE

How's my boy Charlie?

JOE

I don't know. Last week we were thinking we shouldn't have named him after you. He fell out of a treehouse.

CHARLIE

Oh, my gosh! Was he hurt?

JOE

No. He fell on his sister.

CHARLIE

Oh, my gosh!

JOE

It's all right, Charlie. It was a very low treehouse.

CHARLIE

Okay, kid—no more stalling. What are you doing in New York?

JOE

Charlie, what would you say if I brought you a pill that cured the common cold?

CHARLIE

I'd say, "thank you, very much." What is it this time? Analgesic, dehydrator, or vaso-constrictor?

JOE

No, it doesn't deaden, it doesn't dry, and it doesn't shrink. It actually cures.

CHARLIE

Aw—come on, kid.

JOE

No. I mean it.

CHARLIE

Do you know what you're saying?

THE TENDER TRAP

JOE

I know exactly what I'm saying.

CHARLIE

Holy mackerel! Joe, you *really* got it?

JOE

You remember all the trouble we had last year with that new high blood pressure pill? The side effect—those headaches?

CHARLIE

Yeah, I remember. People were wishing they had their high blood pressure back. It's a good thing Van Husen got it out—

JOE

He didn't get it out. I did! Damn near six months in the lab on that one.

CHARLIE

And he takes all the bows!

JOE

Doesn't he always? Ah, the hell with him. Listen to me, Charlie. Six months I worked on that pill, and during those six months Indianapolis was having an epidemic of colds like they never had. Everybody was down—including Ethel and the kids. But I mean *down*— But me—not a sniffle. And nobody else in my lab either—*not a sniffle!* Charlie, that stuff in the high blood pressure pill—the stuff that was causing the headaches—the stuff *I* got out—it cures the common cold.

13

CHARLIE

And the headaches?

JOE

I fixed that too.

CHARLIE

Man, you're in! When are they going to give you a key
to the executive washroom?

JOE

They're not going to give me anything. Van Husen says
the pill won't work. I *know* it will. I proved it over and over
again in the lab, but he says no.

CHARLIE

Why?

JOE

He didn't think of it—it won't work.

CHARLIE

You mean he won't even let you run a field test on it?

JOE

Hell, no.

CHARLIE

Well, what are you going to do?

JOE

I already did.

14

CHARLIE

Did what?

JOE

Quit.

CHARLIE

(*Incredulous*)

What? (*The kitchen door opens and out comes* POPPY MATSON. JOE *regards this dish with unconcealed admiration. He follows her progress across the room.* CHARLIE, *however, pays her no mind*) What do you mean, you quit? You actually walked out? You just got up and quit your job—I don't get it. You been building this spot out there for ten years now, you got the house, you got Ethel, you got the kids—

(JOE *hasn't heard a word* CHARLIE'*s been saying.*)

JOE

(*To* POPPY)

Hello.

POPPY

(*To* JOE)

Hello. (*To* CHARLIE) Sweetie, I'm sorry to interrupt, but it's nearly seven.

CHARLIE

Is it? Gee, that's a shame. . . . Oh, Joe, this is Poppy Matson. Poppy, Joe McCall.

POPPY

How do you do.

JOE

Miss Matson.

CHARLIE

(*To* POPPY)
Well, thanks for dropping by.

POPPY

(*To* CHARLIE)
Sweetie, just before I leave, why don't I tidy up the place a little bit?

CHARLIE

(*Starts to lead her toward the door*)
Oh, no, honey—that's all right.

POPPY

Well, at least let me straighten out the desk.

CHARLIE

That's all right, honey. You do it some other time. And thanks a million for coming over, I'll give you a bell real soon.

POPPY

Tomorrow?

CHARLIE

No—not tomorrow, but soon.

POPPY

You call me.

CHARLIE

I will.

POPPY

On the telephone.

CHARLIE

Yes.

POPPY

Soon!

CHARLIE

That's right—soon. (*Opens the door*) 'Bye.
(*They kiss.*)

POPPY

'Bye. Oh, Charlie, did I tell you? My uncle caught a
whitefish.

CHARLIE

What?

POPPY

My uncle up in Canada. He caught a whitefish.

CHARLIE
(*Urging her out*)
Well, bully for him.

POPPY

Don't you remember? You told me how much you liked
whitefish. My uncle is sending one down.

17

CHARLIE

Oh—grand.

POPPY

I'll call you the minute it arrives.

CHARLIE

You do that. 'Bye.

POPPY

And we'll have a wonderful dinner with burgundy and candlelight and a damask tablecloth and lemons.

CHARLIE

I can hardly wait. 'Bye.

POPPY

(*Another kiss*)

'Bye.

(*Goes.*)

CHARLIE

(*To* JOE)

Now, what do you mean you quit?

POPPY

(*Reappearing*)

I can't bring burgundy! Red wine with meat—white wine with fish!

(*She goes.*)

JOE

Where the hell did she come from?

CHARLIE

What do you mean you quit?

JOE

(*Still wondering about* POPPY)

What? Oh, I just quit, that's all. Look, are there any more around here?

CHARLIE

I don't get it. After ten years, you just walked out.

JOE

Yeah. Look, Charlie, that gorgeous girl—

CHARLIE

Never mind that girl. What does Ethel think?

JOE

What do you think Ethel thinks? Did you ever see a woman who wanted to take a chance?

CHARLIE

What are you going to do now?

JOE

I'm going into business for myself.

CHARLIE

With what?

JOE

With the cold pill—and you. And that girl, if she can type.

CHARLIE

What are you talking about?

JOE

Look. Charlie, you know I'm a careful guy. I didn't even walk into the old man's office till I had over a hundred pages of reports on this new drug. He looks at the first page and says, "It ain't worth a dime." . . . "Well, it's worth more than a dime to me," I say, and I buy it from him!

CHARLIE

You're *that* sure of it?

JOE

I cashed in my bonds, my savings, and my insurance. That's how sure I am.

CHARLIE

Well—what's the plan?

JOE

First we do the field tests, and then we start production. I'll run the factory, you run the sales department. Deal?

CHARLIE

Deal! Are you kidding? We'll make millions! I always knew I was meant to be rich. I can see it all now. Me, sitting on my yacht in my Sulka shirt, smoking my Upmann cigars, drinking my Haig and Haig Pinch, throwing twenty-dollar gold pieces to the native boys— The money. Where's the money for the tests coming from?

JOE

The Van Husen Pharmacal Company of Indianapolis, Indiana.

CHARLIE

How do we work this swindle?

JOE

Well, you've always tested our new drugs out at that Long Island college—what's that guy's name?

CHARLIE

Lindquist—

JOE

Yeah. Good chemist. . . . You take Lindquist the stuff, tell him it's something new the company's working on. He'll run the tests—

CHARLIE

The stuff works, we set up shop, we're rich! (*He pours* JOE *another drink*) Man, you should have gone on the sauce long ago. Brain food.

JOE

Now, the faster we get going, the better. How soon can you get Lindquist started?

CHARLIE

Tomorrow.

JOE

How about tonight? I mean, just to explain it to him.

CHARLIE

Oh, no, it's Saturday night. I've got a date.

JOE

I haven't.

CHARLIE

Well—all right, I'll call him and see. (*He goes to the phone, looks up a number, dials*) You know, this may be the last number I ever dial with this finger. . . . From now on, I'll hire a dozen girls for this kind of menial work—a different girl for every exchange—one Butterfield, one Lackawanna, one Plaza. (*Into phone*) Earl? This is Charlie Reader. How are you? . . . Good. How's all the little test tubes? . . . Attaboy. Look, Earl, Joe McCall from the home office just got here with a rush job for you. What are you doing tonight? . . . Got a date, huh? Well, all work and no play— How about tomorrow morning? . . . Yeah, I know it's Sunday, this is very important. . . . Fine! Come up to the apartment for breakfast. . . . Oh, one o'clock. Your lab assistant? Sure, bring her along. . . . See you tomorrow. Good-bye. (*He hangs up, turns to* JOE) We gotta have breakfast before they get here. That assistant of his—ugliest woman I ever saw.

(*The doorbell rings.*)

JOE

He didn't sound suspicious?

CHARLIE

Why should he? It's coming through channels. (CHARLIE *opens the door and admits a very decorative lady named* JESSICA COLLINS, *aged somewhere between thirty and thirty-*

five, beautifully groomed, smiling pleasantly, and carrying a big round cheese) Hello, Jessica.

JESSICA

Hiya, honey.

CHARLIE

Look, baby, I'm a little busy. . . .

JESSICA

(Deep South accent; nonstop delivery)

Oh, that's all right, darling, it's just that I wanted you to have this. I happened to be down in Washington Market today and I ran right smack into this wonderful real Wisconsin Colby, and I knew you said you liked it better than any other cheese, and so here it is. How *can* you live in a place that looks like this?

CHARLIE

Jessica, this is Joe McCall. Jessica Collins.

JOE

Miss Collins.

(He appraises her admiringly.)

JESSICA

How do you do, Mr. McCall. Have you ever seen anyone keep a place in this disorder? I don't know what Mr. McCall will think. Now you two pay me no mind and go right on talking, and I'll at least have this place looking tidy, my goodness. *(She starts straightening the desk)* Now this is not the way to get a house in order. What this place needs is a

23

real thorough old-fashioned cleaning. A lick and a promise won't do, no sir! Those drapes have to be taken down and simply flogged. That floor wants a good waxing. That couch —what *have* you been doing on that couch? But what am I standing around for? There's no time like the present, I always say.

(*She falls to work.* CHARLIE *restrains her.*)

CHARLIE

Jessica—

JESSICA

Remember I get to keep all the coins I find in the couch.

CHARLIE

Jessica, I appreciate this, but not tonight. We'll get together real soon.

JESSICA

Oh, you always say that!

CHARLIE

No, really. Soon.

JESSICA

Don't forget now, hear?

CHARLIE

I won't.

JESSICA

(*To* JOE)

Good-bye, Mr. McCall. (*She grabs* CHARLIE *and gives him a large kiss*) Tiger!

(*She goes.*)

JOE

Where am I, Polly Adler's? Where do all these tomatoes come from?

CHARLIE
(*Indignant*)
Tomatoes! Do these girls look like tomatoes to you?

JOE

Well, no, but—

CHARLIE

For your information, Poppy is a juvenile editor at Doubleday, and Jessica is a buyer for the largest chain of women's stores in the South. Tomatoes! (*The phone rings.* CHARLIE *picks it up*) Hello. Oh, hiya, honey. . . . No, I can't tonight. No, not tomorrow either. . . . No, the place is *very* clean. . . . Thanks for calling, kid. . . . What? . . . Of course I do. . . . You know I do. . . . Just busy, that's all. . . . Yeah, I'll get back to you. 'Bye.
    (*He hangs up.*)

JOE

Boy, tell me something. What have you got?

CHARLIE

It ain't what I got, it's what I ain't got—a wife.

JOE

A wife?

CHARLIE

It's fantastic. When I first came to New York I figured it would be like home—you call a girl, you take her to the movies, you bring her flowers and candy—you know—romance her.

JOE

Well?

CHARLIE

Boy, was I wrong? . . . You know how it works in New York? There's some kind of underground. The minute a bachelor sets foot in this town, signals go out. I think they do it by radar. Before you get your bag unpacked, you're up to here in women. It's wonderful. Look—a plain joker like me—I got dames I ain't even used yet.

JOE

But what kind of dames?

CHARLIE

That's just it! Fabulous dames. You saw a couple of them —good-looking, intelligent, successful—

JOE

Tidy.

CHARLIE

Tidy, well-dressed, educated, mature—

JOE

And it goes on like this all the time?

CHARLIE

All the time.

JOE

Well, I'll be damned. And all you've got to be is not married?

CHARLIE

That's it.

JOE

Boy! All these folks back in Elwood who said you'd never amount to anything—wait till I tell 'em about this.

CHARLIE

It's nothing, really.

JOE

Nothing, he says. . . . Pal, you really got it taped.

CHARLIE

No, it's not me. It's New York. I tell you this city is *teeming* with dames. If you want to know the truth, I get a little tired sometimes.

JOE

I feel for you, pal.

CHARLIE

Oh, hell, you know what I mean. Sure it's fun, but let's face it—*you're* the one who's got it taped. I'd trade this rat race in a minute for your setup. You come home at night—the nice little house—the three kids running up the path yelling, "Daddy! Daddy!"—and you go inside and there's Ethel in a cute little apron and she gives you a smack and she says—

27

JOE

We've got to have wall-to-wall carpeting.

CHARLIE

Now, don't knock Ethel to me.

JOE

Knock her? Why if it wasn't for Ethel, I wouldn't have wall-to-wall carpeting today. Can you imagine that? People would actually be able to see the floor around the edge of the rug.

CHARLIE

Ugh!

JOE

And, incidentally, the kids don't run down the path at night. They're too tired—after a day of dancing lessons and fencing lessons and dramatic lessons and *finger-painting* lessons. And the fact is, Ethel isn't home either. The dog is taking her to obedience school.

CHARLIE

Aw, come on, kid. It can't always be like that.

JOE

No, no. Some nights after the kids are in bed, it's nice and quiet, just the two of us. I build a fire, Ethel goes and gets the good brandy, we push a couple of chairs together. I squeeze her hand, she squeezes mine. "Honey," I say. "Darling", says she, "don't you think it's time Peter had braces on his teeth?" . . . One stinking kid left in the house without braces, she can't stand it.

CHARLIE

I'm not even listening to you. I can't believe that Ethel—little starry-eyed Ethel with that angel's smile and the cutest little figure in the entire Middle West—(*He looks inquiringly at* JOE) Is it still—

JOE

Yup.

CHARLIE

Now, don't tell me that doesn't please you any more.

JOE

It delights me. Married eleven years and I've never looked at another woman.

CHARLIE

Are you thinking of looking now?

JOE

Certainly not. Why?

CHARLIE

I dunno, when guys start telling me how many years they didn't, I know they're ready to *do*.

JOE

No, no, no, I'm here on business.

CHARLIE

Yeah, yeah, yeah, but that ain't all. You're drinking whisky; you didn't used to do that. You're knocking Ethel; you didn't used to do that. . . .

JOE

I am *not* knocking Ethel.

CHARLIE

Well, what do you call it?

JOE

I haven't said one word against Ethel. She's a fine woman —a typical American housewife—a monster! Look, why do you think I quit my job?

CHARLIE

Why, Old Man Van Husen—

JOE

No—no—I stood him for ten years. I could have stood him for another ten. That wasn't it. It was the money. I was boxed; I couldn't get another dime out of that place . . . and Ethel had to have more. A fine woman, you understand. No bitchery, no screaming—just a few tears and a flick of the whip now and then. . . . So here I am in New York pulling a shady deal. Me, Honest Joe McCall . . . For only one reason—Ethel! Well, maybe when she gets every room carpeted wall to wall, maybe when she joins every club in town, maybe when she puts wire on every tooth in every mouth, maybe then she'll want something else in the house —me.

CHARLIE

Hey, you sound a little frantic. Tell you what, you and I are going to have a real man-to-man . . . (*Looks at watch*) Oh, oh!

JOE

What's the matter? Night shift coming on?

CHARLIE

Listen, I'd rather be with you than— Well, as a matter of fact, I wouldn't. (JOE *laughs*) No, if it was just one of the girls—but this is something really special.

JOE

What's she got—her own vacuum cleaner?

CHARLIE

No, this one hardly cleans up at all. . . . Of course, she straightens out a *little*—but—

JOE

I see. Well, what is it with her? She prettier than the others?

CHARLIE

Well—

JOE

Smarter?

CHARLIE

Well—

JOE

Well—what then?
  (*The doorbell rings.*)

CHARLIE

You'll see for yourself—'cause here comes Sylvia now. (CHARLIE *opens the door, and there stands an extremely handsome woman in her early thirties. She is wearing an evening dress and a mink stole. The first look at this lady tells you that* CHARLIE *was speaking the truth when he said she was something special. She combines dignity and warmth; humor and bearing.* CHARLIE *regards her with a big loving smile, but she does not respond in kind. She surveys him with a conspicuous lack of friendship)* Sylvia, baby!

SYLVIA

This is a tuxedo?

CHARLIE

Now, look honey, I . . .

SYLVIA

Good night.
> (*She goes out, closing the door firmly.*)

JOE

This one *is* different.

CHARLIE
> (*Confidently*)

She'll be back.
> (*The door opens and* SYLVIA *walks in.*)

SYLVIA
> (*To* JOE)

Did he tell you I'd be back?

JOE

Well, yes—

SYLVIA

What's your name?

JOE

McCall.

SYLVIA

Do you have a tuxedo, Mr. McCall?

JOE

Not with me.

SYLVIA
(*To* CHARLIE)

Get ready, boy.

CHARLIE

Five minutes, so help me.
(*He goes into the bedroom.*)

SYLVIA

Can I fix you a drink, Mr. McCall?

JOE

Allow me.

SYLVIA
(*Surprised*)

Such gallantry in this apartment?

JOE

Scotch?

SYLVIA

Fine . . . . (*She muses for a second*) No tuxedo, huh?
. . . Tell me, have you got a blue suit?

JOE

Yes, ma'am! (*He flips open his suitcase*) See?
(SYLVIA *sees a framed portrait of* JOE's *wife and children.*)

SYLVIA

I see.

JOE

My wife and kids.

SYLVIA

Oh, you're *Joe* McCall. I'm Sylvia Crewes.

JOE

Hello.

SYLVIA

That negligee that Charlie sent Ethel last Christmas—did it fit?

JOE

You bought that? I should have known. Charlie wouldn't have that much taste. . . . Yes, it fit fine.

SYLVIA

Charlie gave me very careful directions. "She's about this size," he said. . . .
(SYLVIA *holds out her hands about the width of a woman's shoulders.* JOE *puts his hands on* SYLVIA's *to measure.*)

JOE

Yup, he's right.
(*They laugh, then realize their hands are touching. They draw apart quickly.*)

SYLVIA

(*Looking at the photo*)
Nice-looking kids. Which one is Peter?

JOE

The one without the braces.

SYLVIA

You know, Charlie makes good use of your kids in his courtship—I use the term loosely.

JOE

What do you mean?

SYLVIA

Oh, whenever he gets a little misty he starts telling big lies about some day he wants a nice little wife and nice little kids and a nice little house just like good old Joe.

JOE

Did it ever occur to you that he wasn't lying?

SYLVIA

Mr. McCall, if it hadn't occurred to me I wouldn't be here. (*Knocking on* CHARLIE's *bedroom door; calling*) Forty-five seconds.

CHARLIE

(*Through the door*)
Be right with you.

SYLVIA

(*Threateningly*)
You better be.

CHARLIE
(*In the bedroom*)

Hey, Sylvia.

SYLVIA

Yes?

CHARLIE
(*Through the door*)

Go on over to the phonograph.

SYLVIA

Yes?

CHARLIE

See that recording on top?

SYLVIA
(*Picking up a phonograph record*)

Yes.

CHARLIE

For you.

SYLVIA

Oh, Charlie, you *are* a darling! Come on out so I can give you a great big kiss! (*To* JOE) Look. Toscanini's recording of "Kikamora" by Liadov.

JOE

I never heard of it.

SYLVIA

Well, I sure did. This was the first time I played with Toscanini. Isn't that sweet of Charlie?

JOE

I didn't know you played with Toscanini.

SYLVIA

I don't think he knew it either. I was in the back row of the second-fiddle section.

JOE

This isn't a gag? You really played with Toscanini?

SYLVIA

Sure. I'm a real good fiddle player.

JOE

I don't get it. What are you doing with Tin-Ear Charlie?

SYLVIA

Wait a minute. He's not such a tin ear. I've been working on him and he's making fine progress.

JOE
(*Incredulous*)

Charlie?

SYLVIA

He just loves "Peter and the Wolf." (*She goes to the door of* CHARLIE's *bedroom and sings the first two bars of "Peter and the Wolf"*) Da, da, da—da, da, da . . .

CHARLIE

(*Sings the third bar from the bedroom*)
Da, da, dee, dee, da—

37

SYLVIA

See? . . . And that wasn't easy for him.

JOE

I know, I know. . . . Well, this is a complete vindication for Miss McFetridge.

SYLVIA

Miss McWho?

JOE

Our fourth-grade music teacher. She always maintained Charlie was not tone deaf—just stupid.

SYLVIA

Do you two go all the way back to the fourth grade?

JOE

Kindergarten.

SYLVIA

Tell me, what was he like then?

JOE

Little.

SYLVIA

My father once said to me, "Never ask a man's best friend about him because he won't tell you. That's why he's his best friend."

JOE

Your father's a wise man. . . . Tell me—what'd you do as a kid?

SYLVIA

Like when?

JOE

Like from five to ten.

SYLVIA

Played the fiddle.

JOE

Ten to twenty?

SYLVIA

Played the fiddle.

JOE

Twenty to—

SYLVIA

Say it.

JOE

(*Tentatively*)

Twenty-eight?

SYLVIA

Thank you very much. . . . Well, I kept on playing the fiddle, and one day I discovered that I was no lady Heifetz. So today I'm a house man.

JOE

A what?

SYLVIA

A staff musician. I work for N.B.C. and I play whatever programs they tell me.

JOE

Sounds like fun.

SYLVIA

It was when Toscanini was there. Now it's a living.
 (CHARLIE *comes out of the bedroom wearing a tuxedo.*)

CHARLIE

Five minutes I said; five minutes it is.

SYLVIA

Seven minutes.

CHARLIE

Nag, nag, nag. Joe, I'd ask you to come along—but I don't want you.

JOE

I don't blame you.

CHARLIE

Enjoy yourself. The place is yours. This couch opens up into a bed. Here, I'll show you. It's very simple. Remove suitcase "A," and pillows "B" and "C" and pull handle "D"—
 (*He fiddles with the couch and makes no progress at all.* SYLVIA *comes over.*)

SYLVIA

May I? (*Opens it instantly and shuts it again.* CHARLIE *looks at her balefully.* SYLVIA *shrugs*) Some people have it; some don't. (*Affectionately to* CHARLIE) But you're awful pretty.

40

CHARLIE
(*Pulling bottles of pills from the desk*)
True. . . . Don't wait up for me, Joe. . . . If you have
any trouble getting to sleep, here's some Seconal. If you
have any trouble staying awake, here's some Benzedrine. If
you can't make up your mind, take one of each. . . . You
know where the booze is. . . . Let's see, is there anything
else?

SYLVIA
Food, possibly?

CHARLIE
Food—of course. Oh, yeah. Let's see what's in the refrigerator. (*He goes into the kitchen, leaving the swinging
door open. He can be seen looking into the refrigerator*)
Let's see . . . Pearl onions, anchovy paste, a lemon—

SYLVIA
Sounds grand. Let's eat here.

CHARLIE
(*Coming out of the kitchen*)
What's the matter with me? Here's a whole cheese.
(*He picks up* JESSICA's *cheese and hands it to* JOE.)

JOE
Man eats like a prince around here.

CHARLIE
I guess that's everything. Come on, let's get going.

SYLVIA
Good night, Joe.

JOE

Night, Sylvia.

CHARLIE

So long, Joe.
>   (*He starts to escort* SYLVIA *out. She stops suddenly.*)

SYLVIA

Just a minute. (*She picks up her recording, rejoins* CHARLIE, *kisses him*) Thank you, darling!

CHARLIE
>   (*To* JOE)

Who ever had it so good?

JOE

Not me.

SYLVIA *and* CHARLIE

Good night.
>   (*They leave. After standing quite a moment,* JOE *stirs. He starts to unpack his bag. He regards his wife's picture for a longish interval. The doorbell rings.* JOE *quickly puts the picture back in suitcase.*)

JOE

Come in.

JESSICA
>   (*Enters*)

Hey! How are you?

JOE

(*Warmly*)

Hello!

JESSICA

Isn't Charlie here?

JOE

No, he just went out.

JESSICA

Oh, what a shame. I had something else for him. I forgot to bring it before. . . . A phonograph record . . . his favorite . . . "Peter and the Wolf."

JOE

I'll give it to him.

JESSICA

No—thank you. I'll come back tomorrow.

JOE

You must live close by.

JESSICA

Right upstairs.

JOE

Well, come on in, neighbor. Have a drink.

JESSICA

No, thank you. I've got dinner on the stove.

JOE

Well, turn it off. We'll go out for dinner.

JESSICA

No, thank you.

JOE

But why not?

JESSICA

Why, Mr. McCall, you're a married man.

JOE

Charlie told you, huh?

JESSICA

As a matter of fact, he didn't.

JOE

You mean you could tell just by looking?

JESSICA

(*Regarding* JOE *as though he were backward*)
Why, of course. . . . Good night.
(*She goes.*)

JOE

(*Utterly crushed*)
Oh . . . Good night.
(JOE *stands sadly for a moment, then goes to continue unpacking as . . .*

THE CURTAIN FALLS

Scene II

The following day, 1:30 P.M.

SYLVIA, JOE *and* CHARLIE *are at the table finishing what is obviously a long Sunday breakfast. The Sunday papers are scattered around the room. For a minute there is no conversation as all three read the paper and drain their coffee cups.*

SYLVIA

More coffee, anyone?

> (*Two arms holding cups appear from behind the newspapers.* SYLVIA *fills their cups.* CHARLIE *and* JOE *withdraw their arms and drink.*)

JOE

Good coffee.

SYLVIA

An amusing, unpretentious blend.

CHARLIE

It's different this week, isn't it?

SYLVIA

Yes. . . . But I didn't think *you'd* notice. I thought your taste buds would be burned out after last night.

JOE
(*To* CHARLIE)

What'd you drink?

45

CHARLIE

Tequila.

JOE

What for?

SYLVIA

These friends of ours—the Prescotts—are on a Mexican binge. They spent three days in Tijuana and now you can't see the furniture for the serapes. And Pedro here was lapping it up . . . especially the tequila.

CHARLIE

They taught me how to drink it native style. You know the bit. You take some salt and a piece of lemon. You put the salt on the back of your hand. Then you lick it. Then you drink the tequila. Then you suck the lemon.

(*He demonstrates in pantomime.*)

JOE

Is that good?

CHARLIE

The tequila's no good, but I'm crazy about lemon and salt.

SYLVIA

(*To* CHARLIE)

Have you got the music section of the *Times?*

JOE

Not him!

SYLVIA

Oh, here it is.
 (*She takes paper across the room and sits.*)

JOE

Shouldn't Lindquist be here by now?

CHARLIE

Relax. He'll be here soon.

JOE

But it's past one.

CHARLIE

Don't worry, he'll be here.

SYLVIA

 (*Exploding at something she's read in the paper*)
Pestalozzi!!

CHARLIE

Huh?

SYLVIA

How do you like that! They signed Pestalozzi as conductor of the Duluth Symphony!

CHARLIE

Shocking!

SYLVIA

I don't say he's a bad violinist—but *conductor!*

47

CHARLIE
(*Still not looking up*)
Ridiculous . . . The bum never hit .300 in his life.

JOE
(*Also not looking up*)
Sucker for an inside curve.

SYLVIA
He's good enough with the classics, but what will they do when they get past Brahms?

CHARLIE
They'll have to put in a pinch hitter.

SYLVIA
(*Absorbed; not realizing she's being needled*)
They wouldn't hire a woman for the job—oh, no, of course not—

JOE
Makes it so tough in the locker room.

SYLVIA
(*Realizing she's been had*)
Very funny. . . . What did you two do for laughs before I came along?

(JOE *and* CHARLIE, *as one man, do the idiot bit with the fingers and the loose lips.* SYLVIA *retreats behind her newspaper.* JOE *and* CHARLIE *simultaneously reach for the coffee pot.*)

CHARLIE
Go ahead.

48

JOE

No, you.

CHARLIE

There's about a cup here. We can split it. There's no need to make fresh coffee.

JOE

No, you take it.

CHARLIE

No, you. A fellow can always get along without coffee, I guess.

JOE

What did you say, Charlie?

CHARLIE

I said a fellow can always get along without coffee, I guess.

SYLVIA

(*Rises and walks to table*)
Okay. Okay—I'll go make some more.

CHARLIE

Thank you, darling—you're a doll.
(*As she reaches for the coffee pot,* CHARLIE *grabs her arm and kisses the inside of her elbow.*)

CHARLIE

You know this is a very neglected place on a girl—the inside of her elbow?

49

JOE

Neglected? Why, months go by when I don't touch any other part of a girl.

CHARLIE

(*He is now munching on her wrist*)
How are you on wrists, Joe?

JOE

Oh, they're all right, but I'm an elbow man, myself.

SYLVIA

(*To* CHARLIE)
Look, are you in the mood for coffee or do you want to sit here nibbling on my arm all day?

CHARLIE

Sylvia, there aren't many girls I'd say this to, but—

SYLVIA

I know. You want coffee.
(*She takes her arm and the coffee pot and goes into the kitchen.*)

CHARLIE

Well, how do you like this one?

JOE

What's not to like?

CHARLIE

Damn right. Wonderful girl. Comes up every Sunday morning to fix breakfast, makes the best coffee in the world, pretty as a picture, talented—I'll tell you something. The day I get feeble and decide to marry one of the dreamboats that come sailing in here, she could very well be it.

JOE

You thinking about getting married?

CHARLIE

Me? Now, that's pretty silly, isn't it?

JOE

Yes, it is.

CHARLIE

Why would I throw away a setup like this?

JOE

I don't know, Charlie. Why'd you keep falling out of the treehouse?

CHARLIE

Look, pal, I haven't fallen out of a treehouse in years. Don't worry about old Charlie.

JOE

Now, that has a familiar ring. "Don't worry about old Charlie." Isn't that what you used to scream as you fell over the edge?

CHARLIE

You still think I'm a goof, don't you?

JOE

You are if you throw away this setup.

CHARLIE

Look, marriage is the furthest thing from my mind.

JOE

That ain't fur enough. (*The doorbell rings*) Lindquist?

CHARLIE

Must be.

JOE

I'll get the stuff.

CHARLIE

(*Crossing to door*)

Now don't look directly at his assistant if you can help it. This is one of the truly ugly women of our generation. (CHARLIE *opens the door. Standing there is a lovely thing named* JULIE GILLIS. JULIE *has many attractions, chief among which is the fact that she is twenty-two years old*) Hello.

JULIE

Mr. Reader?

CHARLIE

Yes.

JULIE

I'm Mr. Lindquist's assistant.

JOE

Why, Charlie, I don't think she's so ugly.

CHARLIE

I don't think she's the least little bit ugly.

JULIE

Thanks. I think you're both very pretty too.

CHARLIE

Come on in. What's your name?

JULIE

Julie Gillis.

CHARLIE

Miss Gillis, this is Mr. McCall from the home office.

JULIE

How do you do.

JOE

Hello.

JULIE
(*To* JOE)
What made you think I'd be ugly?

JOE
(*Pointing to* CHARLIE)
My near-sighted friend. He said Lindquist had an ugly assistant.

CHARLIE

He *did.* What happened to that other girl, thank goodness?

JULIE

Miss Spangenburg? She got married.

CHARLIE

(*Shrugging*)

It's possible.

JULIE

Mr. Lindquist is parking the car. He'll be right up.

CHARLIE

Won't you sit down?

JULIE

(*Sits*)

Thank you. (*Addresses* JOE) Mr. McCall, I have been waiting a long time to meet you.

CHARLIE

You have?

JULIE

Yes—I have you to thank for my career.

JOE

How's that?

JULIE

You remember last year when Mr. Lindquist was running that field test on Permahist?

JOE

Yes.

JULIE

Remember sending him a letter that you needed one more test—a female in her twenties who was allergic to egg white?

JOE

Yes.

JULIE

Well, that's me. I'm twenty-two. I'm female.

CHARLIE

Yes!

JULIE

And—allergic to egg white—all I have to do is to look at an egg and I blow up like a balloon. So I went over to the lab and you know something? I'd never been inside a lab before. I took one look around and said to myself, "What am I doing in English Lit? Compared to this, Chaucer is nowhere!"

JOE

And the Permahist cleared up your allergy, huh?

JULIE

Not a bit.

CHARLIE

Quiet. I sell a million capsules a year.

JULIE

Well, that's all right. If people think a drug's going to help them, it probably does. It's all in the mind anyhow.

JOE

This is a very subversive little girl.
(SYLVIA *comes in from the kitchen.*)

SYLVIA

Hello.

CHARLIE

Oh, Sylvia, this is Miss Gillis . . . Miss Crewes.

BOTH

How do you do.

CHARLIE

Miss Gillis is Mr. Lindquist's assistant over at the university. They try out all our new drugs on people.

JULIE

Well, not people exactly—students. My, you certainly have made this place attractive. It didn't look like this the last time I was here.

CHARLIE

(*Incredulous*)
You have been *here* before?

JULIE

Oh, this was a long time ago—once when we were looking for an apartment. Daddy and I saw this one. We were crazy about it.

CHARLIE

You mean you actually lived here?

JULIE

No. Mother saw it and she said, "This is no place for a family. This is for an old bachelor who's chasing young girls."

(*This amuses* JOE *and* SYLVIA, *but not* CHARLIE.)

CHARLIE

Lindquist is on his way up. How are we fixed for coffee?

SYLVIA

Coffee we've got. Cups are the problem. Too bad we can't serve the coffee in Pimms Number One cups. The old bachelor's got two dozen of those.

(*She starts to pick up cups.*)

JULIE

Can I help?

CHARLIE

No, thanks. You just stay here and be decorative.

SYLVIA

And *you* just come along and be useful!

(*Exits to the kitchen with coffee pot.* CHARLIE *takes chair and coffee pot and plate and starts for kitchen.* JOE *gets two cups and saucers and the newspapers from the table, and starts for the kitchen.* CHARLIE *turns back to* JULIE, *still holding the chair.* JOE *continues out the kitchen door.*)

CHARLIE
(*To* JULIE)

I'll be right back. Don't go away!

(*The doorbell rings.*)

JULIE

That's Earl. I'll get it.

CHARLIE

(*Puts down the chair*)

Thanks. (*Going out kitchen door*) Joe—Mr. Lindquist is here!

(JULIE *opens the door, and* EARL LINDQUIST *stomps in.*)

EARL

(*Snarling at* JULIE)

Why didn't you wait for me?

JULIE

(*Sharply; fearing the others might hear*)

Shh!

EARL

(*Unheeding; furious*)

I was gone for three minutes. Couldn't you wait?

JULIE

(*Snapping*)

Earl!

EARL

Three lousy minutes!

JULIE

Take off your hat!

(JOE *comes out of the kitchen.*)

58

JOE

Mr. Lindquist? I'm Joe McCall.

EARL

(*Shaking hands*)

Hi.

JOE

Hi. I've been looking forward to meeting you. You know, you saved me three months lab work on Osmacydin? That was as nice a piece of reasoning as I've ever seen.

EARL

It was pretty obvious.

JOE

Yeah? Well, it got past everybody in *our* lab. . . . That's why I'm so glad to have you on the new project.

EARL

What have you got?

JOE

A cold pill.

EARL

(*Deprecatingly*)

Oh, no! Not another one.

JOE

This one is different. It works. . . . I've got all the information in my brief case. Give me a minute and I'll dig it out. . . . Sit down. Coffee'll be here right away.

EARL

(*Glaring at* JULIE)

We're not staying for coffee.

JULIE

I would like some coffee.
(JOE *goes into bedroom.*)

EARL

(*Angrily*)

You're real agreeable this morning.

JULIE

(*Coldly*)

Thank you. You're pretty sweet yourself—screaming at me all the way down here.

EARL

Well, that's the only way to get anything through that hard head of yours.

JULIE

Please, Earl. This is not the place for an argument.

EARL

I don't care what place it is. Why can't you make up your mind? Why can't you give me a straight answer?

JULIE

What could be straighter than *no?*

THE TENDER TRAP

EARL

You haven't thought it through.

JOE

(*Coming out of bedroom with papers and jar containing his new drug*)

Now here's the way it goes.

(JOE *spreads the papers on the table.*)

EARL

Is this the stuff?

JOE

Yeah. Now, this is the first precipitation test. You'll notice that—

(EARL *opens the jar. He dips in his little finger, picks up a dab of the stuff, and tastes it with the tip of his tongue. He smacks his lips thoughtfully, like a professional wine-taster.*)

EARL

(*To* JOE)

What's the active ingredient?

JOE

There are two, and they're synergistic. Here, I'll show you. (*He unfolds a large sheet of paper, points first at one side and then at the other*) Here—and here.

EARL

Well, what do you know! Nobody ever thought of that before. Do they combine all right?

JOE

Combine? They're locked in a death-grip. (*He holds up his hands, locked in a grip, for emphasis*) If you really want to go nuts, try and separate them.

EARL

(*With a look at* JULIE)
No, I'm nuts enough now—people tell me.

JULIE

What have you got on lab animals?

JOE

(*Indicating three sheets in turn*)
Dogs—rabbits—monkeys.

JULIE

Well, you *have* done a lot of work.

JOE

(*To* EARL)
That's why I don't think this should take you too long. Do you suppose two weeks might do it?

JULIE

Oh, easy!

EARL

Now, wait a minute! Mr. McCall, if you want me to do this test, then you've got to let me do it my way.

JOE

Of course.

EARL

It might take two weeks, it might take three, it might take six.

JOE

Six!

EARL

I can't tell you now. But I can tell you this: I don't like people breathing down my neck. . . . Okay, Mr. McCall?

JOE

Okay, okay.

EARL

Okay. I guess it won't take too long. It happens right now I can give it full time. . . . But don't be calling me. I'll call you when I'm ready.

JOE

Fine. Just take your time.

EARL

I will. (*To* JULIE) Come on, Madame Curie.

JULIE

(*Not moving*)

Madame Curie is staying for coffee.

(EARL *glares at her. The kitchen door opens and out comes* CHARLIE, *carrying coffee pot.* SYLVIA *follows with cups, cream and sugar.*)

63

CHARLIE

Soup's on!

JULIE

My, that smells good.

SYLVIA

(To EARL*)*

Hello, I'm Sylvia Crewes.

EARL

Hiya.

JULIE

It would never occur to him to tell you, but his name is Earl Lindquist.

SYLVIA

How do you do.

EARL

Hiya.

CHARLIE

(To EARL*)*

How soon do you think you can finish the test?

EARL

Now, look here—

JOE

(Interrupting smoothly)

That's all straightened out. Mr. Lindquist's going to give us full time on this job.

CHARLIE

Well, sir, if I had somebody like Miss Gillis in my office,
I'd give my job full time too.

(*This sally pleases* SYLVIA *not at all.*)

EARL

Miss Gillis, are you coming?

JULIE

No, I am not coming.

EARL

Miss Gillis, I would like you to come.

JULIE

And I would like some coffee.

EARL

All right, if you're that fond of coffee, you can take a
taxicab!

(EARL *exits.*)

CHARLIE

(*To* JULIE)

Lover's quarrel?

JULIE

Me and Earl? Are you serious?
(*She laughs, indicating that the whole notion is too
ridiculous.*)

CHARLIE

Well, it did look a little like—

65

JULIE

No, no, nothing like that. It's just that Earl's the excitable type.

SYLVIA

(*To* JULIE)

Sugar and cream?

JULIE

No—just black, thank you.

JOE

You'd never know he was excitable from his reports. I'd have guessed that he was a very sober and thorough young man.

JULIE

He is—in the lab. . . .

JOE

Even with you beside him?

JULIE

Oh, sure. The minute we get in the lab, I'm just the girl who takes notes—and pretty good ones, if I say so myself.

CHARLIE

You like your work, huh?

JULIE

Oh—it's all right—but only temporarily.

SYLVIA

Are you thinking of taking up something else?

66

JULIE

Oh—yes. . . . Marriage, I hope.

SYLVIA

I see. . . . But not Earl?

JULIE

Heavens, no!

CHARLIE

Then there's some other young man?

JULIE

There are any number of other young men, but I haven't found mine yet.

CHARLIE

Well, a pretty young thing like you won't have any trouble.

JULIE

I certainly hope not. I mean, a career is fine, but it's no substitute for marriage. Don't you think so, Miss Crewes?

SYLVIA

Miss Gillis, I think so. . . . Passionately, I think so.

JULIE

What is your career, Miss Crewes?

SYLVIA

I'm a violinist.

67

JULIE

Oh, how thrilling. . . . You mean you give concerts and stuff like that.

SYLVIA

No, I'm not a soloist.

JULIE

Oh . . . you play in a band.

SYLVIA

Yes. Toscanini's band.

JULIE

Toscanini! Oh, I think that's just dreamy!

SYLVIA

Well—it keeps me off the streets.

JULIE

Yes. . . . Well, of course . . . But, honestly, don't you think marriage is just the most important thing in the world? I mean, a woman isn't really a woman at all until she's married and had children. (*She picks up the framed picture of* JOE's *wife and children*) Look at her, for instance. (*To* CHARLIE) Your wife?

CHARLIE
(*Hastily*)
No, no. No, no . . . Joe's wife.

JULIE

Well, look at her . . . just beautiful! I'm sure she was a pretty girl . . . but look at her now among her children.

68

She's *beautiful*, really *beautiful!* And why? Because she's *fulfilled!* Isn't that right?

CHARLIE

Right!

JOE

(*To* CHARLIE)

You agree?

CHARLIE

What red-blooded American boy doesn't?

JOE

This red-blooded American boy doesn't.

JULIE

Why not?

JOE

Well, in order to be fulfilled you need a man . . . and it's just possible that what fulfills you may not fulfill him.

JULIE

My man it will.

JOE

Oh, you know all his specifications?

JULIE

Do I? I! I know everything except his blood type.

CHARLIE

Well, tell us about it.

JULIE

Do you really want to know?

CHARLIE

More than anything in the world.

JULIE

You mean it? Because this is something I could talk about all day.

SYLVIA

You're on, Miss Gillis.

JULIE

Well—the first thing I want in a man—he's got to love children.

CHARLIE

How many did you have in mind?

JULIE

Three.

JOE

That's the magic number, all right.

JULIE

But not right away. The first two years we're going to live in New York. I mean we'll be young and we'll want to have fun, and there's no better place to have fun than New York, is there? The children will come later.

CHARLIE

But not in New York?

70

JULIE

No, we'll move to the country for that.

SYLVIA

I see.

JULIE

Well—probably the first baby will be born in New York.

JOE

What hospital?

JULIE

Doctors— Oh, you're kidding me.

CHARLIE

Never mind him. We really are interested.

JOE

Fascinated.

SYLVIA

Now you've lived in New York for two years and you've had your first baby—

JOE

At Doctors Hospital—

JULIE

Yes . . . and now we buy a house in the country.

JOE

Split-level?

71

JULIE

Yes— Look, do you want to hear this or don't you?

SYLVIA

Joe, do we have to send you out of the room?

CHARLIE

Yeah!

JOE

I'll be good.

CHARLIE

Now you're in the country, you've got the house and the baby—now what do you do?

JULIE

I have two more babies.
(*A slight pause while they all look at* JOE.)

JOE

I didn't say anything.

CHARLIE
(*To* JULIE)

Yes?

JULIE

Well, when the children get out of the Scarsdale public schools—

SYLVIA

Oh—Scarsdale?

JULIE

Certainly. Everyone knows they have the best school system in the country.

JOE

Sure, everybody knows that.

SYLVIA

Now, Joe—

JOE

Well, they do. I mean back in Indianapolis everybody's sending their kids to Scarsdale.

JULIE

Okay. That does it.

CHARLIE

You go right ahead. Don't you pay any attention to that old needler.

JULIE

I've been kidded about this before, but I know what I want.

CHARLIE

That's right. You go on.

JULIE

Well, I was saying, when the children get out of high school and go off to college—

73

JOE

Miss Gillis, forgive me. Aren't you figuring things out just a little bit far ahead?

JULIE

Well, after all, a person can't just go on ad-libbing his way through life.

JOE

Some do.

SYLVIA

Some have to.

JULIE

Yes, but that's because they made their plans too late. Well, now that I've told you all of my girlish dreams—
(She rises.)

CHARLIE

Oh, wait a minute. You're not going?

JULIE

I have to.

CHARLIE

So soon?

JULIE

I really have to.

CHARLIE

Stick around. We're all going to make fudge later.

THE TENDER TRAP

JULIE

Gee! That sounds keen, but I've got to go. Honest.

CHARLIE

I'll take you down and get you a cab.

JULIE

Don't bother. I'll find one.

CHARLIE

Why, I wouldn't dream of letting a mother of three children out alone on the streets of sinful old New York.

JULIE

Thank you. Good-bye, Miss Crewes, Mr. McCall.
(*She goes.*)

SYLVIA *and* **JOE**

Good-bye.

CHARLIE

I'll just go down and get her a cab.
(*He goes.*)

JOE

That is the most terrifying child I ever saw in my whole life.

SYLVIA

I'm a little shaky myself.

JOE

Now wait a minute. Are you worried? A girl like you— sweet, intelligent, charming, talented, beautiful, exciting

. . . (*He stops, realizing he's been carried away*) You know, I haven't talked like this in twelve years?

SYLVIA

Well, for Heaven's sake, now that you're started, don't stop.

JOE

I have to. You're Charlie's girl.

SYLVIA

Am I?

JOE

Well, anyhow, you're not mine . . . I regret to say. (*There is a tiny pause.* SYLVIA *reaches for a cigarette. He lights it for her*) Here.

SYLVIA

Thank you.

JOE

You're welcome.

SYLVIA

She's *something*, that little Miss Gillis.

JOE

She sure is. (*Mimicking*) Tell me, Miss Gillis, what are your plans for the next four hundred years?

SYLVIA

(*Going along with the gag*)
Well, first I shall have some children.

JOE

Oh, bully! And how will you have them?

SYLVIA

The usual way.

JOE

No, I mean in what order?

SYLVIA

Oh . . . First a boy, then a little girl, then another boy, then a chocolate cream.

JOE

And what typical little American community will you live in?

SYLVIA

Las Vegas, where else?

JOE

Natch. And what would you like in a husband—besides a ring in his nose?

SYLVIA

(Laughs)

Joe, this is a dandy game, but I've got a rehearsal. The boys in the band are waiting to do the "Eroica" bit. So I'll just pile the dishes in the sink and go out in the streets of sinful old New York and get a cab all by myself.

JOE

Hey, I've never seen a rehearsal. Any chance of my going?

SYLVIA

Well, not today—but what are you doing on Wednesday night?

JOE

Biting my nails.

SYLVIA

Let me find out this afternoon. I'm sure I can arrange it.

JOE

That'd be great. . . . And I get to buy you a dinner before the rehearsal.

SYLVIA

You get to buy me a tunafish sandwich and a malted milk at the lobby drug store, which is where I'll meet you.
(*She starts to pick up the coffee cups.*)

JOE

Here, I'll help.

SYLVIA

Don't bother.

JOE

No bother. (*They go into the kitchen.* CHARLIE *comes in the front door. He goes to the desk, writes* JULIE's *name and number on a slip of paper, and spindles it.* JOE *returns. He closes the kitchen door*) Well, what's she doing in 1978?

CHARLIE

Huh?

JOE

The little commissar with her fifty-five-year plan.

CHARLIE

Boy, you really don't know anything about women, do you?

JOE

I know this one. She's a trap—with the trigger all set.

CHARLIE

Aah!

JOE

Let an old battle-scarred veteran give you some advice. Keep the hell away from women who know what they want.

CHARLIE

Listen, she's just a cute, confused little girl.

JOE

Yeah? With her whole life all mapped out?

CHARLIE

My friend, she doesn't even know what she's doing next Wednesday night.

JOE

(*Pained*)

Oh, Charlie, you didn't—
    (SYLVIA *comes out of the kitchen.*)

CHARLIE

(*Quickly; to* JOE)

Shh!

(SYLVIA *picks up her purse and gloves.*)

SYLVIA

I'll see you, Joe. Charlie—(*She gives him a fast kiss*) thanks for letting me fix your breakfast. . . . You're one hundred percent, kid.

CHARLIE

So long, honey. I'll be in touch.

SYLVIA

(*Pausing at the door*)

Charlie, how would you like to come to a rehearsal next Wednesday night?

CHARLIE

Wednesday night? Now, let's see. . . . Gee, kid, I'm sorry. Joe and I have to go to a meeting of the Pharmacological Institute Wednesday night. Don't we, Joe?

JOE

(*Tonelessly*)

Yeah.

SYLVIA

(*She is not deceived*)

I see. So long.
(*She goes out.*)

JOE

(*Shaking his head*)

Well, it's comforting to know that some things never change.

CHARLIE

Like what?

JOE

Like you being an idiot. . . . You know, you had me fooled for a while. When I came here and saw this setup, I said to myself, "Can this really be Charlie? Can this really be old Charlie with the two left feet? Has he really got it made this time?"

CHARLIE

What'd I do?

JOE

Are you figuring to add that little Gillis girl to your collection?

CHARLIE

Well, I made a date with her.

JOE

Oh, no!

CHARLIE

Why not? She's a cute kid. All she needs is a little straightening out.

JOE

And *you* are going to straighten *her* out?

CHARLIE

Sure. (JOE *brushes imaginary twigs off* CHARLIE's *shoulders*) What are you doing?

JOE

Charlie, my boy, you just fell out of the treehouse again. (*As* CHARLIE *looks at him in bewilderment . . .*

THE CURTAIN FALLS

ACT TWO

ACT TWO

Six P.M., *Saturday. Three weeks later.*
JOE *is talking on the telephone.*

JOE

Yes—Yes—I'll tell him. (*Hangs up, writes message, spindles it, and starts for bedroom. The telephone rings. Answering*) Hello? . . . No, he's not. . . . Miss Who? . . . Sri, did you say . . . Spell it. . . . S-R-I. (*He writes the name on the pad beside the phone, muttering as he writes*) What the hell kind of a name is that? (*Into the phone he says:*) Yes, Miss Sri. . . . United Nations . . . a curry dinner . . . next Thursday night . . . I'll tell him. (*He hangs up the telephone, spindles the note, and starts back to the bedroom. The phone rings before he has gone three steps. He answers*) Just give me the facts, ma'am. . . . Oh, hello, Poppy. How are you? (*Writes* POPPY's *name on the sheet, tacks it up.* CHARLIE *comes in through the front door. He is carrying a brief case*) No, Poppy, he's not here yet. (CHARLIE *nods approvingly at* JOE's *lie. He throws down the brief case*) Really? I'm sure he'll be very happy. I'll tell him the minute he gets in. Good-bye.

(*He hangs up.*)

CHARLIE

Hiya, Joe?

JOE

Hiya, Stud?

CHARLIE

(*Going over to table and looking at his mail*)
What's Poppy want?

JOE

What do they all want? To feed you, caress you, burp you,
sew monograms on your shirts.

CHARLIE

(*Riffling through his mail*)
Oh, did Carol get the monogram thread?

JOE

(*Consulting the bulletin board*)
Yes, she did . . . in three colors. . . . And Poppy Matson got that whitefish from her uncle in Canada, and a Miss
. . . S-R-I . . . of the United Nations wants you to come
over and curry her on Thursday evening.

CHARLIE

(*Amiably*)
Thank you very much, and you'll find a little something
extra in your pay envelope next Saturday.

JOE

I hope you don't mind—I tied up your phone for three
minutes this afternoon with a personal call. Ethel phoned.

CHARLIE

How is she?

JOE

She says she's restless and bored and she's going to carpet the bathroom. Also she wants to know what I've been doing here for three weeks—and frankly, I'm beginning to wonder the same thing.

CHARLIE

Take it easy, boy. Lindquist is doing just fine, Julie says.

JOE

Sure, he's doing fine, considering that he's running the whole thing by himself. Why don't you get Julie home early enough so she doesn't fall asleep in the lab?

CHARLIE

Oh, she's young—great recuperative powers.

JOE

Recuperative powers, hell. If she'd been doing her work properly, Lindquist would have been through by now.

CHARLIE

Relax.

JOE

(*Getting more and more worked up*)

Why do you have to romance this little girl anyhow? In the first place, she's made out of cast iron, in the second place, she's too young for you, and in the third place, you've got more dames than you know what to do with now.

CHARLIE

And in the fourth place, you've got a little trouble yourself. I've been watching it develop, boy. The symptoms are classic—short temper, jangled nerves, rude to your friends and loved ones. . . . Son, what you need is a woman.

JOE

Thank you very much, Doctor. Now how about Lindquist? When is he gonna finish?

CHARLIE

I don't know. Soon, I suppose. But why mope around here all day long? Go on out and do yourself some good.

JOE

Aah!

CHARLIE

Come on. It's Saturday and the town is full of obliging ladies. Don't sit around here tonight all by yourself.

JOE

(*A little hesitantly*)
Well, as a matter of fact, I'm not.

CHARLIE

(*Delighted*)
Good boy! Got a date, huh? (JOE *nods*) Who is she? Anybody I know?

JOE

Sylvia.

CHARLIE

(*This news pleases him not a bit. For an instant his smile vanishes, but he puts it back and forces a hearty tone*) Huh? Oh, great! Great!

> (*He goes over and starts riffling through his mail again.*)

JOE

You did that.

CHARLIE

Oh. (CHARLIE *stops fiddling with the mail. Casually*) Did she call you?

JOE

No, I called her. Now there's a switch.

CHARLIE

Oh.

> (JOE, *fully aware of* CHARLIE'S *agitation, applies the needle with bland, evil deftness.*)

JOE

What's the matter, Charlie?

CHARLIE

Nothing, nothing.

JOE

But?

89

CHARLIE

Well, I just think you ought to know that if it's action you want, you'll get nowhere.

JOE

I didn't figure to.

CHARLIE

Well, just so you know.

JOE

All right. Now I know.
(*There is a pause.* JOE *watches him with cool, impassive eyes.*)

CHARLIE

Sylvia's a lot of laughs. You'll have fun.

JOE

That's the general idea.

CHARLIE

(*Going to the bar*)
Where you taking her?

JOE

No place, We're spending a quiet evening at home.

CHARLIE

How can you? She lives in a woman's hotel.

JOE

I know. I'm bringing her back here.

CHARLIE

Here!
(*He slops whisky all over the bar.*)

JOE

It's all right, isn't it? You're going out?

CHARLIE

Yeah. Sure.

JOE

Well, I knew you'd want me to feel perfectly at home here.

CHARLIE

Sure, sure.

JOE

It's a perfect place to bring a girl.

CHARLIE

(*Facing* JOE *with the friendliest of smiles*)
Joe, you know I'm a broad-minded fellow.

JOE

I know.

CHARLIE

I mean, I'm not stuffy or anything like that.

JOE

I know, I know.

CHARLIE

Well, I don't think you should see Sylvia.

JOE

Why not?

CHARLIE

Because you're a married man.

JOE

(*Amused*)

You are the greatest! Three minutes ago you were telling me to pick up the first woman I saw. Now you tell me I'm a married man.

CHARLIE

A one-night stand—all right—that's got nothing to do with Ethel. . . . But a girl like Sylvia—that's different.

JOE

How?

CHARLIE

A girl like Sylvia—you get involved. This girl is not interested in a slap and a tickle. This girl has got marriage on her mind. . . . Have you?

JOE

Have *you*?

CHARLIE

Well, at least I'm in a position to. You're not.

JOE

Aren't you taking this pretty big? All I want from the girl is a nice, pleasant, companionable evening.

CHARLIE

(*Triumphantly*)

Companionable! See? It's started already! . . . This girl's a charmer, I tell you. You won't be satisfied with *one* nice, pleasant, companionable evening. You'll want more and more. You'll get *involved*.

JOE

(*Mocking gently*)

Like you are, huh? Oh, she's really got her hooks in you. She gets to come up here and fix breakfast for you every Sunday morning—and brings her own bagels.

(*The telephone rings.* CHARLIE *wants no part of it. He looks appealingly at* JOE.)

JOE

No. Get it yourself.

CHARLIE

(*Into phone*)

Hello . . . oh, hello, Poppy. Now, isn't that funny? I was just picking up the phone to call you. . . . Yes, I heard about the whitefish. That's pretty exciting. . . . What? . . . Well, I don't know just when I'll be able—what? . . . Well,

93

can't you freeze it? . . . Fine, I'll call you. . . . Huh? . . .
Why, sweetie, you know I do. . . . Just busy, that's all. . . .
I'll get back to you, doll. . . . Good-bye.

(*Hangs up and turns to find* JOE *staring at him.*)

JOE

Charlie, a thought occurs to me. You are a first-class
louse.

CHARLIE

(*Incredulous*)

Me?

JOE

You're not gonna call her back, you're not gonna see her,
you're not gonna eat her whitefish. Why don't you let the
poor girl go?

CHARLIE

Who's holding her?

JOE

You are—holding her and Miss S-R-I of the U.N. and that
nutty one who brings you cheese—and Sylvia. All dangling
on a string while you run around with little Julie Gillis.

CHARLIE

I'm not holding any of them. I have made no offers, no
promises of any kind. And as far as you're concerned I'd
appreciate a little consistency, pal. You're the one who
told me I had it all taped. Now you tell me I'm a louse.

JOE

The louse of the world. I believe you're one of the few really *indecent* men I've ever met.

CHARLIE

Don't you take a high moral tone with me—you with a wife and three kids—what are you going out for tonight?

JOE

Why, company.

CHARLIE

Hah!

JOE

And you're the guy who talks about consistency.

CHARLIE

I'm consistent.

JOE

Sure . . . you say to me—me, a married man with three kids—you say, "Go on out and get some action"—that's all right—but not with Sylvia—that's all wrong—because she won't give you any action—but if she does, that's all wrong too because I've got a wife and three kids, which you knew very well when you sent me out tomcatting in the first place. Consistency!

CHARLIE

You're twisting my words.

95

THE TENDER TRAP

I'll twist your arm, you silly jerk! You want to keep me away from Sylvia? Just do one simple thing. Marry her.

CHARLIE

(*As though marriage were some strange occult custom*) Marry her?

JOE

You bet. This is a *lady*—a first-class, A-Number-One, triple-distilled lady. This is no trophy to keep in your game room; this is a girl to marry!

CHARLIE

Marry! Marry! All you married guys are the same. Just because you're hooked, you want everybody else hooked, too. . . . No, sir. You said it right in the first place; I've got it taped. . . . I know it and you know it.

JOE

Okay, Charlie . . . and I've got a date and you've got a date, so let's get ready. (*He starts for the bedroom, but just before he goes through the door, he turns and says quietly:*) You'd be the luckiest guy in the world if she'd have you. (*He goes into the bedroom.* CHARLIE *is profoundly disturbed. He goes over to the bar. As he is about to mix a drink, the doorbell rings. He walks to the door and opens it. Standing there is* JULIE GILLIS. *In his agitation,* CHARLIE *fails to notice how pretty she looks. He greets her abstractedly*) Oh. Hi, Julie. Come on in. (*He starts back to the bar. But she doesn't come in. She stands expectantly at the door, wait-*

ing to be kissed. CHARLIE *turns, notes her condition, goes back and kisses her—but with no great enthusiasm. Again he starts away. She detains him.*)

JULIE

Come back here. You can do better than that.

CHARLIE
(*Grinning suddenly*)

Yes, I can.
(*He does.*)

JULIE

There. That wasn't so bad, was it?
(CHARLIE *nuzzles her cheek, then sniffs and pulls back.*)

CHARLIE

Hey! Who are you? You don't smell like Julie Gillis.

JULIE

Don't you remember the perfume that funny Mr. Billingsley gave me?

CHARLIE

Oh, yes. Did you put it where I told you?

JULIE

Uh-huh. (*She lifts the inside of her elbow for his inspection. He sniffs it approvingly. At this touching moment* JOE *comes out of the bedroom in a blue suit.* JULIE *sees him,*

quickly withdraws her elbow from CHARLIE. *Embarrassed*)
Hello, Mr. McCall.

CHARLIE

(*Also embarrassed*)

Oh, hi.

JOE

Hello, Miss Gillis.

CHARLIE

Got time for a drink?

JOE

No, thanks. (*To* JULIE:) You wouldn't happen to know
how Lindquist is coming along?

JULIE

Fine, I think. He's doing a very thorough job—even for
Earl. I've never seen him run so many tests.

JOE

That's swell. . . . I hope it won't be too much longer.

CHARLIE

(*With sarcasm*)

Joe's in a big hurry to get back to his family.

JOE

Good night, Miss Gillis. (*To* CHARLIE) Do you want me
to phone before I come back?

98

CHARLIE

It won't be necessary. We'll be gone in fifteen minutes. The place is all yours.

JOE

Fine.
  (*He starts out.*)

CHARLIE

Just a minute. You wouldn't mind taking a little message along? Tell your friend the Sunday breakfast is out.

JOE

I'll deliver your message.

CHARLIE

Julie and I are going riding tomorrow morning.

JULIE
  (*Ecstatic*)

Oh, Charlie!
  (JOE *and* CHARLIE *exchange glares.* JOE *exits.* JULIE *rushes to phone and starts dialing.*)

CHARLIE

Who are you calling?

JULIE

The stable. You have to make reservations in advance. Gee, I hope they're still open.
  (*As she waits for the phone to be answered, she*

99

glances at the notes on the bulletin board—phone messages from CHARLIE'S *harem.* CHARLIE *rushes over to distract her.*)

CHARLIE

Julie! . . .

JULIE

What's the matter?

CHARLIE

(*Kissing her nose to draw her attention away from the bulletin board*)
Nothing. You're cute, that's all.

JULIE

So are you. (*As she kisses him back, he reaches behind her and surreptitiously tears the evidence off the bulletin board.* JULIE *speaks into the phone*) Hello, Ben? This is Miss Gillis. I'd like to reserve two horses for tomorrow morning . . . eight o'clock.

CHARLIE

Whoa, Tonto!

JULIE

(*To* CHARLIE)
What's the matter?

CHARLIE

That's a little early, isn't it?

JULIE
Nine?

CHARLIE
Eleven.

JULIE
(*Into phone*)
Make that nine-thirty, Ben . . . and, Ben, I'd like to get the same horse I had last time . . . that darling with the long white mane—Silver. . . . Now just a minute. (*She addresses* CHARLIE) What kind of horse would you like?

CHARLIE
A dignified, elderly animal.

JULIE
(*Into phone*)
Can Queenie still get around? That's right—Silver's mother! Fine, Ben. Her too. 'Bye. (*Hangs up*) Let's not be late, Charlie, because they only hold the horses for ten minutes.

CHARLIE
All right. I'll meet you at the stable at precisely 0930. Synchronize watches.
> (*He lifts his wrist, but she doesn't go along with the gag.*)

JULIE
Darling?

CHARLIE

Yes?

JULIE

Couldn't you call for me?

CHARLIE

What's the point? You're all the way uptown—the stable is on 66th—it would only waste time.

JULIE

Look, dear, I haven't complained before, but do you think I like it—picking you up here—meeting you at restaurants? Don't you think I'd be happier if you called for me?

CHARLIE

But that's crazy. Here I am in the sixties—you're way out in Hell and Gone. . . .

JULIE

(*Indignantly*)

Hell and Gone? 92nd Street is a very nice neighborhood.

CHARLIE

I yield to no man in my admiration for 92nd Street, but why waste all that time?

JULIE

Well, for one thing, my mother would like it better. (*Wryly*) She still has some old-fashioned notions about chivalry.

CHARLIE

I don't understand. What's this all about?

JULIE

Look, I know this is the atomic age and we are two civilized adults. You made that clear. But a girl still doesn't like to call for a man at his apartment or meet him at a bar. . . . Especially when the whole evening has been planned without consultation.

CHARLIE

Consultation?

JULIE

That's right. Every date we've had has been all figured out by you. You've never asked me once—*not once*—what *I* wanted to do.

CHARLIE

Honey, baby, why didn't you tell me? I'm sorry. Tell you what, we'll make a big change right now. What do you want to do tonight?

JULIE

Well, I don't know.

CHARLIE

We've got the whole town . . . Anything you say.

JULIE

Gee, I don't know. What do you want?

CHARLIE

Oh, no. This is *your* evening.

JULIE

Well—
　　(*She ponders.*)

CHARLIE

Take your time. (*He waits patiently while she ponders some more*) May I make a suggestion?

JULIE

Oh, please!

CHARLIE

Well, I thought—if you like, of course—that we might go down to a Spanish restaurant where they have the very best *paella Valenciana* in the whole world and afterward—I mean, if you want to—just a couple of blocks away there's a joint where they play rhumbas like you never heard in your life. . . . And then we'll go to a place on 14th Street, and get some real, genuine espadrilles with rope soles. Then we're going to pad right across the street to a café where they serve the best coffee and guitar music in town.

JULIE

Charlie, the next time I tell you I want to plan an evening, just don't listen.

CHARLIE
　　(*Laughing, kissing her*)

I won't.

JULIE

Because you know more about how to please a lady than any other human male on the eastern seaboard.

CHARLIE

Thank you. And there's no lady I'd rather please.

JULIE
(Curtseys)

Thank *you.*

CHARLIE
(Bows)

Thank *you.*

JULIE

Shall we dance?

CHARLIE

No, let's neck.

JULIE

A very sound idea.
 (They sit on the sofa and exchange a hearty kiss.)

CHARLIE

You know, I've been meaning to tell you something for days. You are the softest girl!

JULIE

Flattery will get you nowhere.

CHARLIE

But it's true. You're so young and fresh and, you know, innocent.

JULIE

And if I'm very good, do I get a new Tinkertoy for Christmas?

CHARLIE

I said it wrong. . . . I don't mean you're childish. I mean the way you look at everything. It's so positive and brave, kind of, and starry-eyed.

JULIE

You mean I don't know what the score is?

CHARLIE

That is true. In fact, it's one of the reasons I started going with you. I thought I'd be a good fellow and straighten you out. But I've changed my mind. I'm going to let you keep just what you've got.

JULIE

I appreciate that.

CHARLIE

The great thing about you is that you make *me* feel young too . . . as though there were still a world to win and all you needed was a stout heart and willing hands and the race was to the swift.

JULIE

(*Raising her fist heroically*)

Excelsior!

(CHARLIE *laughs and kisses her.*)

CHARLIE

You kill me. You're just about the most refreshing thing I've seen.

JULIE

I bet you tell that to all the girls.

CHARLIE

(*Earnestly*)

No, I *don't!* I mean they're swell kids, all of them— bright and good-looking and everything—

(CHARLIE *reaches for her but she has grown cool at the mention of his other girls. She spurns his embrace.*)

JULIE

How many are there, Charlie?

CHARLIE

How many what?

JULIE

Those other girls. How many are there?

CHARLIE

Baby, you know better than to ask that kind of question.

JULIE

Oh, I'm sorry. This is a new game to me. I don't know the rules.

CHARLIE

Julie, relax.

JULIE

How many?

CHARLIE

Aw, come on. It's Saturday night, we're going out, and there's nobody in the whole wide world but you and me.

JULIE

And tomorrow?

CHARLIE

Same thing. We're going riding, aren't we?

JULIE

And Monday?

CHARLIE

What do you want—a contract?

JULIE .

All I want is a straight answer to a straight question. How many are there?

CHARLIE

(*Exploding*)

Four hundred and ninety-six. There used to be four hundred and ninety-seven but one of them started asking questions that were none of her damn business.

JULIE

(*Livid*)

Thank you very much.

CHARLIE

Why don't you cry now? That's next, isn't it? First the silly questions, then the silly answer, then the tears. Go on—do the whole bit. I'll go get dressed. (CHARLIE *stalks to his bedroom.* JULIE *goes to the bar and starts to pour herself a drink. He reappears from the bedroom, and shakes a finger at her*) And lay off that booze. You don't know how to handle it.

(*He goes into the bedroom.* JULIE *slams down the bottle. Her face starts to dissolve in tears, but she checks them quickly. With great determination, she pulls herself together. She picks up her purse, takes out a handkerchief, and dabs at her mascara. All at once she stops and looks at the picture of* JOE's *wife and kids. She puts down the picture. She strides over to the bedroom door and bangs on it violently with her fist.*)

JULIE

(*Shouting*)

Come on out here, you! (CHARLIE *emerges from bedroom, looking puzzled. He is in shirtsleeves*) Listen here, God's

109

gift to women, and listen good. From now on you are going to call for me at my house. You are going to ask me how I want to spend the evening. You are going to meet my folks and you are going to be polite to them. And you are going to bring me candy and flowers.

CHARLIE
(*Agog*)

Candy?

JULIE

And you are going to drop every one of those other girls—all four hundred and ninety-six of them!

CHARLIE

Now, why would I do a thing like that?

JULIE

Because I love you.

CHARLIE

(*This logic baffles him*)
Because you . . . huh?

JULIE

That's right—because I love you. Do you think that such a wonderful thing—being in love with you? I never wanted to. I don't want to now. You're selfish, you're arrogant, you're spoiled, you're much too old for me, you—

CHARLIE
(*Interrupting indignantly*)
Now—wait a minute—

JULIE

Shut up. Too old, I said. Too old, too selfish, too spoiled. Lord knows why I love you, but I do. . . . And that's why there's going to be some changes made—right now.

CHARLIE

Listen—

JULIE

You listen. You're very big with your terrace and your Stork Club and your espadrilles—but let me tell you something; you've got a lot to learn about women.

CHARLIE
(*Incredulous*)
Me?

JULIE

Yes! You. . . . And I'm going to straighten you out if it's not too late. I'm going to try to make a man out of you— because that's what I want to marry—a man.

CHARLIE

Marry? Who asked you?

JULIE

Well, what's this all about? (CHARLIE *searches for words*) If you don't intend to marry me, say so now. . . . That's what I want—not a terrace, not pa-la-la Valenciana or whatever the hell you call it—just plain old marriage and a house and kids and a life that makes some sense.

CHARLIE

Are you all through?

JULIE

Yes.

CHARLIE

This, I understand, is an ultimatum.

JULIE

Yes.

CHARLIE

You want me to marry you—(*She nods*) But first you want me to reform—mend my ways.

JULIE

Yes.

CHARLIE

(*The speech starts quietly, but builds in volume*)

All right. Now let a selfish, spoiled, arrogant old man tell you a couple of things. Next time you propose to a man, don't start by calling him a decrepit louse. That won't make him rush you to the nearest altar. . . . Now let's get down to cases. I have never said I want to marry you—nor am I moved to do so now. And assuming I did want to get married I know a girl who comes a hell of a lot closer to my idea of a wife than you do. (JULIE *has heard all she wants. She picks up her things and starts for the door, fighting back tears. She goes out and he shouts the following lines after her as she goes down the stairs*) In fact, I know any number of girls . . . And what's more, they like me just the way I am! (*He slams the door. He mutters angrily*) Any number of girls! (*As he passes a mirror, he notices that his tie is untied. He stops and ties it, muttering aloud as he works*) Damn right. Any number of girls. (*His fingers, shaking with anger, make a mess of the tie. He starts again*) I don't have to sit around here. Not this kid! Any number of girls. (*Again he fails to knot his tie. In his present condition, this final irritation is too much to bear. He runs to the phone, finds and dials a number. He shouts into the phone*) Hello. Countess Mara? When a man comes into your store and pays fifteen dollars for a tie, is it too much to expect the stinking tie to tie? (*Not waiting for an answer, he bangs down the receiver. He tries again with the tie. He shouts at the phone*) Fifteen dollars! I used to buy a suit for fifteen dollars. (CHARLIE *starts to dial another number. The doorbell rings. He opens the door and admits* EARL) Oh, hello, Earl. What's up? You got the report?

EARL

No.

CHARLIE

Oh? Then what do you want?

EARL

I've got to talk to you.

CHARLIE

Some other time, Earl. I'm on my way out.

EARL

No, it's got to be now.

CHARLIE

All right. What do you want?

EARL

I followed Julie.

CHARLIE
(*Warily*)

Oh?

EARL

Yeah, I followed her. And I just saw her come out of here, bawling. I tried to stop her, but she wouldn't talk to me.

CHARLIE

Yes?

EARL

I've made up my mind about something. . . . You're a pretty big fellow, but the way you live, inside it's probably all mush. Anyhow, I'm gonna find out. I'm gonna punch you right square in the mouth.

CHARLIE

(Calmly)

I see. Would you care to tell me why?

EARL

Yeah, I'll tell you why. . . . I was making pretty good progress with this girl. I know she's a hardhead, but I'd have worn her down. Then you had to come along. . . . Big operator . . . I always knew some guy might take her away from me . . . but take her away to *marry*, not for the kind of stuff that you dish out.

CHARLIE

(Thoughtfully)

This is my day all right.

EARL

(Rising)

And that's why I've gotta belt you in the mouth. Get up.

CHARLIE

I wouldn't do that if I were you, Earl . . . for two good reasons. First, because I'll knock you right on your can. And second, because you can have little Julie back with my compliments. (EARL *throws a wild roundhouse right which* CHARLIE *ducks.* CHARLIE *grabs* EARL *expertly and pushes him into a chair. He stands over him, pushing him down whenever* EARL *tries to rise*) Sit down, Earl. You don't know me well enough to give me this much trouble . . . sit down . . . now, before you resume this heartwarming romance with little Julie, you're going back to your lab and do

115

what you're getting paid for. I want that report here for Joe McCall tomorrow morning. First thing, you understand? (EARL *is silent;* CHARLIE *pulls him to his feet*) Understand?

EARL
(*Cowed*)
All right.

CHARLIE
All right . . . and now, boy scientist, get the hell out of here.

> (*He lets* EARL *rise.* EARL *opens the door, and standing in the doorway is the lovely* POPPY MATSON. *In her arms is a large package.*)

POPPY
(*Startled by the suddenly opened door*)
Oh! (*She sees only* EARL) Is Charlie Reader at— (*Now she sees* CHARLIE) Oh, hello, Charlie.

CHARLIE
(*Gleefully; with open arms*)
Poppy, Poppy, you sweetheart!

EARL
You don't waste any time, do you?
> (*He goes.*)

CHARLIE
Poppy, you're a mind reader. How did you know that in all the world there was only one person I wanted to see— and that is beautiful you.

> (*He plants a noisy kiss on her cheek.*)

POPPY

Well!

CHARLIE
(*Taking the package from her arms*)
A present for me? You shouldn't have.

POPPY

I had to.

CHARLIE
(*Opening the package*)
Nonsense. You didn't have to bring anything but your sweet little old self. (*The package is open now and a large dead fish lies in* CHARLIE's *hand*) What the hell is this?

POPPY

Charlie, you know how small my refrigerator is.

CHARLIE
(*Confused*)

Yes?

POPPY

Well, I can't freeze it in there. I've barely got room for a jar of yogurt.

CHARLIE

Oh, this is your uncle's whitefish.

POPPY

No, Charlie, it's *your* whitefish.

CHARLIE

Delighted to have it. You're a doll to bring it. I'll take good care of it.

POPPY

Don't leave it on the table. I wouldn't have come running over here if this could be kept on the table.

CHARLIE

I'll take care of it in a minute. But now let me ask you a question. You are, are you not, the girl who loves *paella Valenciana* better than anything in the world?

POPPY

That's me. I'm the girl.

CHARLIE

And you are, are you not, the girl whose ankles are just made for espadrilles?

POPPY

Yup, that's the kind of ankles I got. You bet!

CHARLIE

And you are, are you not, the girl who goes like this— (*Executes Flamenco handclaps*)—when you hear guitar music?

POPPY

I'm the girl who does it—(*Imitates the handclaps, but not very successfully*) *Ole!*

CHARLIE

Then you must be the girl who's leaving here with me right now and going downtown to eat the Spanish food and hear the Spanish music and buy the Spanish shoes. Yes?

(POPPY *gives* CHARLIE *a playful kiss.*)

POPPY

No!

CHARLIE

No? For Heaven's sake, why not?

POPPY

Because I've got a date with somebody else.

CHARLIE

Well, break it.

POPPY

Break it? Just like that?

CHARLIE

Sure.

POPPY

I see— and then what?

CHARLIE

And then we'll go out and have a ball.

POPPY

Uh-huh. And then what?

CHARLIE

And then we'll come home.

POPPY

Uh, huh . . . and then what?

CHARLIE

What do you mean?

POPPY

I mean like tomorrow, Charlie.

CHARLIE

Will you quit worrying about tomorrow? Look, this date of yours, is he going to take you downtown and buy you espadrilles and *paella Valenciana?*

POPPY

No, he is going to take me to the Radio City Music Hall, and afterward . . . if it isn't too late . . . to Schrafft's!

CHARLIE

So what's your problem? Get rid of the square and let's go.

(*He offers his arm. She fends him off.*)

POPPY

But . . . he is also going to call me tomorrow.

CHARLIE

And that makes him a big hero, huh?

POPPY

It's polite, Charlie. It's gentlemanly.

CHARLIE

What are you saying . . . that I am a louse?

POPPY

Certainly not. I wouldn't dream of calling you a louse.
. . . A heel, maybe. Or a cad. Or . . . what's that other
one? A stinker. That's it . . . Charlie . . . a stinker.

CHARLIE

Thank you very much.

POPPY

Por nada. Take care of the whitefish, darling.

CHARLIE

Well, this is good-bye, then, huh?

POPPY

Why?

CHARLIE
(*Startled*)

Why? After what you just called me . . .

POPPY

A stinker? Why, Charlie, I never thought you were anything else. . . . *Hasta la vista!*

(*Exit* POPPY. CHARLIE *stands gaping miserably. Finally he stirs and walks over to the phone. He dials, then hangs up. He finds himself face to face with the fish.*)

CHARLIE

(*To fish*)

What are you doing tonight?

(*Suddenly overcome with anger,* CHARLIE *grabs the fish by the tail and flings it out through the open French doors that lead to the terrace. But even this defiant gesture affords him no satisfaction; it only covers his hands with slime and scales. Holding his hands gingerly away from him, he goes into the bedroom, on his way to the bath. After a moment the front door opens, and in come* SYLVIA *and* JOE.)

SYLVIA

How did you ever discover this place?

JOE

Just lucky, I guess. (*She starts to put down purse and gloves*) Hey, just a minute. Before you put your purse away, where's your dollar?

SYLVIA

(*Extracting a dollar and laying it on the table*)
Right here. Where's yours?

JOE

Right next to it.

(*Places dollar beside hers.*)

SYLVIA

I feel terrible about this. It's just like stealing money.

JOE

(*Walking over to a shelf behind the bar*)
Never mind feeling terrible. Just leave your money right there.

(*He takes a record off the shelf.*)

SYLVIA

Joe, for one whole year, I studied nothing but Haydn.

JOE

You quit too soon.

SYLVIA

Look. I know every recording that was ever made.

JOE

You do, huh? (*Hands her the record*) What does this say?

SYLVIA

(*Reading label*)
Haydn . . . Symphony No. 63 . . . Berlin Staats oper . . . I just don't believe it!

JOE

Read it again.

SYLVIA

(*Reads label silently*)
I believe it.

JOE

(Picking up money)
That'll teach you to make bets with me.

SYLVIA

But how in the world did you find this?

JOE

That's all I've been doing for the last week—looking through old records.

SYLVIA

But why?

JOE

Trying to find a present for you. I liked the way you thanked Charlie when *he* gave you a record.

SYLVIA

Joe, this is very sweet, but it's also very silly.

JOE

I guess so, but—*(He looks at her amorously)* Sylvia—

SYLVIA

(Warningly)

Joe!

JOE

Look, I can't help it. I—
(He starts for her. At this moment CHARLIE *emerges from the bedroom.* CHARLIE *carries a towel in his hands, abstractedly.)*

THE TENDER TRAP

CHARLIE

(*Speaking more to himself than to the others*)
Sure. This is great, isn't it? This is just fine. Saturday night, and I've got a date with a Turkish towel.

JOE

What are you doing here?

CHARLIE

Is this a way to live? Getting my brains knocked out like this? What am I—a high-school kid or something? Isn't it time my life had a little order, a little sense?

SYLVIA

Charlie, what's wrong?

CHARLIE

I'm nuts, that's what's wrong. I'm blind and stupid and nuts. Why do I keep fighting it? Here you are a first-class A-Number-One triple-distilled lady. What better thing in the world could happen to me? What greater favor could I possibly do myself?

SYLVIA

Charlie, what is it?

CHARLIE

Sylvia, marry me. (SYLVIA *reacts as though hit with a blunt instrument. Without a word she sits down*) You will, won't you?

SYLVIA

I will.

CHARLIE

Good. That's settled. (CHARLIE *nods and stands still for a moment. He's pretty stunned himself. Then, remembering the procedure at a time like this, he kisses* SYLVIA. *She promptly bursts into tears.* CHARLIE *is alarmed*) What are you crying for?

SYLVIA

Don't be alarmed. This is standard operational procedure. (*She goes into the bedroom.*)

CHARLIE

Gee, I never saw her cry before.

JOE

Yeah.
(JOE, *too is a little stunned. He has been in a sort of daze since the proposal.*)

CHARLIE

Aw, she'll stop. . . . She's a great girl, just like you said. . . .

JOE

Uh-huh.

CHARLIE

Yes, sir. This is the smartest thing I ever did. You damn well know it.

JOE

Mm.
(CHARLIE *notices* JOE'S *gloom.*)

CHARLIE

Well, this is a happy occasion. She's in there weeping bitter tears; and you're standing there grunting. Where's the shoes and rice and Roman candles?

JOE

(*Speaks formally, shakes* CHARLIE's *hand*)
I want to wish you all the luck in the world.

CHARLIE

Pal, you do not. You had a big fix on this girl yourself. True?

JOE

True.

CHARLIE

Well, you were right. She's something!

JOE

Tell me, how did you get so smart between five and six o'clock?

CHARLIE

Well, when two hundred and eighty-three people in a row come up and call you a louse, you begin to think maybe there's something to it. . . . Now, I never started out to be a louse, but look what happens. You were pretty impressed yourself when you came here and saw the stuff running in and out of this apartment. Well, think what it did to me when I first came here—a kid fresh out of Indianapolis. I

127

thought I'd died and gone to Heaven! You don't run after girls, they run after you. You don't bring them presents, they bring you presents. A few years of this, you gotta turn into a louse. . . . Well, I've had it, I don't want to be a louse any more.

JOE

What do you want to be now?

CHARLIE

All I want to be is left alone. I don't want nine dames banging my phone and little Julie having fits on my sofa and that mallet-head Lindquist coming up here and throwing punches at me—

JOE

Lindquist was here?

CHARLIE

Yeah.

JOE

Let me see the report.

CHARLIE

He didn't have it. But he'll have it here tomorrow.

JOE

Well, what's he say? Does the stuff work?

CHARLIE

I don't know. I forgot to ask him.

128

JOE

Forgot to ask him!

CHARLIE

What are you worried about? The stuff's gotta be great. (SYLVIA *comes out of the bedroom, composed and smiling.* CHARLIE *rushes over to her*) You all right? (*She nods*) No more crying?

SYLVIA

If you think *that* was crying, wait till you catch me at the wedding.

CHARLIE

(*Thoughtfully*)

I might do a little myself.

JOE

I'm too old to cry. I'll just cut my throat.

SYLVIA

Well, this is a jolly gathering.

CHARLIE

You're right. There's altogether too much gloom around here. . . . Let's get blind. Here's a little something to take the chill off a cold September evening.

> (CHARLIE *picks up a bottle and fills a glass with a huge slug of whisky. He hands the glass to* SYLVIA.)

SYLVIA

A little large, isn't it?

CHARLIE

Come on, kid. Live! How many times you gonna get engaged?

(*She shrugs and lifts her massive drink.* CHARLIE *offers* JOE *a drink.*)

JOE

I'll pour my own. This isn't my party.

CHARLIE

(*Excited*)

Party! That's what we need—a party. Let's have the biggest ball that anyone ever had!

SYLVIA

Party?

CHARLIE

To celebrate! (*He tosses off his drink.* CHARLIE *is obviously trying to whip himself into a gaiety that he doesn't feel*) First we'll call the Prescotts. (*He starts to dial, says to* JOE) Wonderful people, the Prescotts . . . well, actually she's sort of a stiff, but he—well, so is he, for that matter. (*He speaks into phone*) Harry, you old pirate, how the hell are you? . . . Charlie Reader . . . Yeah, I know. I've been busy. . . . Listen, take that wonderful little wife of yours and slip her into something seductive and get right over here. We're having the biggest ball you ever saw. . . . Company? Bring 'em along. . . . Of course we'll feed 'em. . . . I don't care how many. . . . Fourteen? Bring 'em. Attaboy. (*Hangs up*) Well, there's a start.

JOE

You better get some more pearl onions.
(CHARLIE *pours himself another big drink. He's getting more manic by the minute.*)

CHARLIE

Now, let's see. . . . Who else should we have? . . . Hey! Is George Fitzgerald in or out?

SYLVIA

In.

CHARLIE

That's a shame. He plays a wonderful piano.

JOE

You don't have a piano.

SYLVIA

That wouldn't stop George.

CHARLIE

We gotta have some musicians. Musicians are more fun than anybody.

SYLVIA

Sol Schwartz?

CHARLIE

You're a genius! . . . Well, one good thing about Sol— you always know where to reach him. If he's not here, he's not in town. Curley's Bar? . . . Is Sol Schwartz there?

(*Talks to* JOE *while he waits*) Sol's taking the cure—trying to get back on liquor. (*Into phone*) Sol, Dad, *was machst du?* . . . Listen, how would you like to drink some free booze tonight? . . . My place . . . Good man . . . Say, can you get in touch with Eddie and Louise? . . . I know they're with you, but can you get in touch with them? Fine, bring 'em along. . . . What? (*Turns excitedly to* SYLVIA) George Fitzgerald is out!

SYLVIA

There goes the lease.

CHARLIE

Sure, bring him. . . . Okay, Sol. See you . . . Huh? . . . Oh! . . . Charlie Reader! (*Hangs up*) Now we're in business. This is going to be some party. Hey! We're gonna need more booze. I'll go downstairs to the liquor store. This is going to be some party!

(CHARLIE *hurries out.*)

SYLVIA

Poor baby, he's scared stiff.

JOE

Poor baby, he's *getting* stiff.

SYLVIA

Come on, Joe, don't be a sourpuss.

JOE

Me? I'm all right.

SYLVIA

What's the matter?

JOE

Nothing. Why should anything be the matter?

SYLVIA

Come on, what is it?

JOE

It's nothing.

SYLVIA

Look, I don't know you long, but I know you good. What is it?

JOE

Well, damn it, what kind of way is that to act? A girl like you says yes—a man ought to be on his knees—not getting crocked and calling up every bum in town.

SYLVIA

Oh, I don't mind. That's just Charlie's way.

JOE

I don't get it. Anything this guy does is okay with you. Why do you let him shove you around? You're a beautiful woman, you're intelligent, you're talented, you're everything a man dreams about. . . . Why do you stand for it?

SYLVIA

Joe, dear Joe, how can I tell you? We come to this town from Springfield and Des Moines and Fort Worth and Salt

Lake City. We're young and pretty and talented. All we have to do to get married is stay home. But the boys back home don't have what we want. We've got our eyes on something else—a career, glamour, excitement—and this is the place to find it. So we come to New York . . . and we do pretty well. Not great, but pretty well. We make a career; we find the glamour and excitement. We go to first nights, we buy mink stoles, head waiters call us by name . . . and it's fun, it's wonderful . . . till one fine day we look around and we're thirty-three years old and we haven't got a man.

JOE

But surely you—

SYLVIA

(*Interrupting*)

Huh-uh. Do you know what's available to a thirty-three-year-old woman? Married men— (*She points at* JOE) drunks, homosexuals, pretty boys looking for somebody to support them, lunatics looking for their fifth divorce . . . Quite a list, isn't it? . . . So when a sweet guy like Charlie comes along—eligible, attractive, employed, reasonably sane—

JOE

But how much will you take?

SYLVIA

Whatever is necessary. . . . Look, I know what's been going on these last few weeks. I know all about little Julie. But curiously enough, she only made me feel more hopeful. . . . Because I knew that when Charlie started chasing this child, he was just about ready for wedding bells. And I hoped—God help me, I'm not ashamed to say it—I hoped he'd have so much trouble with this little hardhead that I might catch him on the rebound. . . . And I did.

JOE

(*Without enthusiasm*)

Well then—congratulations.

SYLVIA

Thanks.

(JOE *looks morose. She goes over and kisses him in a sisterly manner. At this moment* CHARLIE *enters carrying paper bags containing liquor.*)

CHARLIE

(*Jocularly*)

Out of the house two minutes and you find your best friend smoking your cigars, drinking your brandy, and kissing your wife.

(SYLVIA *goes over to assist him with his package.*)

SYLVIA

Here, let me help.

CHARLIE

Careful, don't waste a drop—that's Old Smuggler. (*He sets down the bag and extracts a bottle of Old Smuggler*) Thought I was kidding, huh? (*He pulls out a bottle of Beefeater Gin*) And look here—nothing but the best—Beefeater Gin. (*He holds both bottles by the necks and clinks them to-*

gether while he sings) The bells are ringin' for me and my gal. . . .

> (*The doorbell rings.* CHARLIE *goes to the door and opens it. There stands* JESSICA, *holding a big round cheese, just as in Act One.*)

JESSICA

Hi, Charlie. I just happened to be down at the Washington Market again and— (*She notices the others in the room*) Oh.

CHARLIE

Come in, come in. (*He pulls her into the room*) Jessica, I want you to meet my fiancée. Miss Crewes, Miss Collins.

SYLVIA

How do you do?

JESSICA

(*To* SYLVIA)

How do you do?— (*She stands in stunned silence for a moment. Then to* CHARLIE) Your *what?*

CHARLIE

Fiancée.

JESSICA

You mean you're engaged?

SYLVIA

Yes.

JESSICA

To be married?

SYLVIA

Yes.

JESSICA

*(She nods her head sadly for a moment, then she takes the
cheese from* CHARLIE *and hands it to* SYLVIA*)*
A wedding present!

SYLVIA

Thank you.

CHARLIE

Jessica, we're having the damnedest party here tonight
and you're cordially invited.

JESSICA

Thank you, Charlie, but I've got a date with some of the
girls for dinner.

CHARLIE

Girls? Bring them here.

JOE

Hell, yes.

JESSICA

No, thank you, I don't believe I will.

CHARLIE

Come on. We're going to really live it up.

JESSICA

No.

CHARLIE

Everyone's going to get blind.

JESSICA

Well—on second thought, yes.

CHARLIE

Good girl! See you later!

JESSICA

Congratulations, Miss Crewes. Charlie, I hope you'll be very hap— (*She can no longer resist. She gives* CHARLIE *a big kiss*) Tiger!
(*She exits.*)

CHARLIE

You know, she's a buyer for one of the biggest women's chain stores in the South. Food— Hey, we'll need some food, won't we?

JOE

With thirty-two people coming to dinner? What for?

SYLVIA

I'll go get some things.

138

CHARLIE

That's it. You and Joe go on up to Barney Greengrass. I'll stay here and get the bottles open. (SYLVIA *extends her palm;* CHARLIE *looks at it blankly for a moment, then realizes she wants money to buy the groceries*) Oh, yeah. (*He takes a wad of bills out of his pocket*) Get all kinds of wonderful stuff—caviar, turkey, sturgeon—all kinds of stuff. . . . Will a dollar be enough?

> (*She laughs. He laughs. He gives her a handful of money.*)

SYLVIA

I'll see you in about an hour.

CHARLIE

I'll count the minutes.

JOE

There should be sixty.

SYLVIA

> (*Kissing* CHARLIE)

Tiger!

> (SYLVIA *and* JOE *go out.* CHARLIE *resumes unpacking the liquor. He takes two bottles out by their necks, sets them on the bar. He lifts out another two bottles, stands for a moment, holding them aloft. He clinks them together, sings.*)

CHARLIE

The bells are ringin'— (*He stops singing. Suddenly he sags—face, shoulders, body. The spirit has gone entirely out of him. In anguished tones he says*) What have I gone and done?

> (*He collapses, the very picture of misery. After a moment the door opens and* JULIE GILLIS *comes into the room. Her entrance is shy and tentative.* CHARLIE *rises. They hold still for a second, then she runs to him.*)

JULIE
> (*Sobbing in* CHARLIE's *arms*)

I love you.

> (*They kiss passionately as* . . .

THE CURTAIN FALLS

ACT THREE

ACT THREE

The next morning.
There is nobody visible as the curtain rises. The apartment shows ample evidence of last night's revels—dozens of glasses containing the dregs of drinks, ash trays full of butts, furniture overturned and askew. The sofa is opened into a bed; it stands rumpled with blankets thrown back.

JOE
(Rising from behind the bar)
Isn't there one lousy clean glass in the place? (JOE *is carrying a bottle of tomato juice. He starts groping around, looking for a clean glass. He draws the drapes to get more light for his search. A blast of sunlight sears his eyeballs and he cries out like a wounded animal, throwing his arm over his eyes. After a moment he recovers and resumes his search for a clean glass. He finds one that looks fairly clean, then puts it down. He gives up looking for a glass, and drinks the tomato juice out of the bottle.* CHARLIE *emerges from his bedroom. He looks even more hung over than* JOE. JOE *offers him the tomato juice, but he shakes his head. Instead he lurches to the bar and pours himself a stiff jolt, which he cannot bring himself to drink. Then he sinks onto the bench and buries his face in his hands.* JOE *starts searching the room for a cigarette. He opens a couple of cigarette boxes, but finds them empty.)* Got a cigarette?

CHARLIE

I don't smoke.

(*Then* JOE *starts to lift what looks like the lid of a cigarette box, which turns out to be one end of a concertina. The instrument emits a horrible squawk, causing both* JOE *and* CHARLIE *to run for cover.*)

JOE

I don't remember anybody playing a concertina last night.

CHARLIE

George Fitzgerald.

(JOE *finds a longish butt in an ash tray, straightens it out and lights it.*)

JOE

Well, son, you did it. You had the damnedest party anyone ever saw. (CHARLIE *grunts;* JOE *chuckles reminiscently*) I haven't played "Run, Sheep, Run" in years. . . . (*He chuckles some more*) Where'd you ever get the idea Sue Prescott was stuffy? I can't think of many girls who'd let George Fitzgerald give 'em a crew cut. (*He laughs again.* CHARLIE, *however, is notably morose*) Hey, who was that girl in the Turkish shoes? (*He curls his fingers to indicate turned-up toes*) I think I'm engaged to her.

CHARLIE

Joe, I did something terrible last night.

JOE

Ordering those parakeets? Oh, hell, a fellow can always use a dozen parakeets.

CHARLIE

No, listen, Joe, I did something really awful. (CHARLIE *pauses, girding himself to speak. Meanwhile* JOE *is folding away his sofa-bed. As he lifts up the bed, the figure of a small, fat man is revealed, lying on the floor. He is clutching a trombone.* CHARLIE, *alarmed*) Oh!

JOE

Sol Schwartz!

SOL

Man, I thought you'd never get here.

CHARLIE

You all right?

SOL

(*Rising*)

Crazy, man. (*He holds out his hand*) Lay it on me. (CHARLIE *makes him a drink, which* SOL *tosses off at a gulp*) Crazy party.

JOE

(*Grinning*)

Crazy.

SOL

Where's Sylvia?

CHARLIE

Home.

SOL

What you mean . . . home?

CHARLIE

Home . . . Her place.

SOL

I don't dig . . . You're engaged, ain't you?

CHARLIE

Yes.

SOL

And she still sleeps at home?

CHARLIE

Yeah, Sol.

SOL

Man, you gotta be crazy to let that chick go home, and I don't mean crazy like cool. Don't you let her go home no more.

JOE
(*To* SOL)

I'm with you.

SOL

She is the most.

JOE

The end!

SOL

(*To* JOE)

What band you with?

JOE

I'm with the Van Husen Pharmacal Company.

SOL

(*Sympathetically*)

Whatsa matter, man? Lose your lip?

JOE

No, I never was a musician.

SOL

What do you do?

JOE

I make pills.

SOL

(*Very interested*)

Yeah? You make bennies?

JOE

Bennies?

SOL

Benzedrine, man. Benzedrine! The staff of life.

JOE

Yeah, we make it.

SOL

Do you use testimonials?

JOE

I'll ask them when I get back.

SOL

Yeah. (*To* CHARLIE) You *really* let that Sylvia go home?

CHARLIE

Yes, Sol.

SOL

You shouldna. This is a real gone doll. How'd she ever get on that Beethoven kick?

CHARLIE

Sol, didn't you say you had a rehearsal this morning?

SOL

Yeah . . . the Longine Symphonette. And for that you gotta be on time. They all got watches.

CHARLIE

One for the road?

SOL

Thanks.
  (*He takes a whole bottle, puts it in his pocket, exits.*)

CHARLIE

Joe, listen, there's something . . .

JOE
(*Interrupting*)
Funny little guy, that Sol. But he knows what's what.
Your Sylvia . . . she *is* the most. I've thought so from the
beginning, but last night . . . that look in her eyes . . .
that wonderful shining look . . . she was a happy woman.
. . . You keep her that way, hear?

CHARLIE
(*Miserably*)
Yeah . . . Listen, Joe, I've got to tell you something. I
did something so awful last night. . . .

JOE

Who didn't?
(*The doorbell rings.* CHARLIE *answers it. In comes*
JULIE.)

JULIE

Hello.

JOE

Hello . . . Where's Lindquist?

JULIE
(*Uncomprehending*)
Lindquist?

149

JOE

Didn't you bring the report?

JULIE

What are you talking about? (*She turns to* CHARLIE *and speaks sharply*) Why weren't you at the stable this morning?

CHARLIE

But, Julie, don't you remember? You were going to call me if you felt well enough to go riding.

JULIE

Call you? I've been trying to get you on the phone for three hours.

CHARLIE

What? The phone never rang. Did it, Joe.

JOE

No.

JULIE

I called you twenty times!

CHARLIE

(*Wishing to distract Julie*)
Isn't that funny. Maybe something's wrong with it. (*He picks up the phone to listen for the dial tone. As he lifts it, we see that the cord has been severed. He says thoughtfully*) George Fitzgerald.

150

JULIE

(*Looking around the room*)
What's been going on here?

CHARLIE

(*Changing the subject*)
How do you feel this morning? (*To* JOE) Julie was pretty
sick last night—lumps and blotches all over her.

JOE

She looked all right when I saw her.

JULIE

What went on here last night?

CHARLIE

Oh, nothing. . . . How about some coffee?

JOE

Yeah, Charlie, what went on here last night?
(*The doorbell rings.*)

CHARLIE

Well, I wonder who that can be?
(CHARLIE *hands* JOE *the phone, and runs to the door
like a man reprieved.* SYLVIA *enters.*)

SYLVIA

Hello, darling.

CHARLIE

Oh. Hello.
> (*He extends his hand for a handshake. She gives it a shake.*)

SYLVIA

Hey! (*Now that this joke is over, she pulls him to her and gives him a big fat kiss. She has not yet seen* JULIE, *but she notices* JOE, *over* CHARLIE's *shoulder*) Hi, Joe.

JOE

Hi.

SYLVIA

What's the matter with your phone? I've been trying to call all morning.
> (JOE *holds up the phone, showing the severed cord.*)

JOE

George Fitzgerald.

CHARLIE

> (*Extricating himself from* SYLVIA's *arms*)

Julie, you remember Sylvia.

SYLVIA

> (*Noticing* JULIE *for the first time; speaking coolly*)

Oh, yes. Hello.

JULIE
> (*Also coolly*)

Hello.

CHARLIE

Well, what brings you here so bright and early?

SYLVIA

(*To* CHARLIE)

Did you by any chance find a diamond earring around here this morning—and please say yes.

CHARLIE

A diamond earring?

JOE

No.

SYLVIA

Oh, that's terrible. Sue Prescott is going out of her mind. When she couldn't reach you she started calling me at seven o'clock—and Harry screaming at her all the time. . . . (*Imitates gruff male voice*) "It isn't bad enough you let that lunatic shave your head, you had to let him steal your earring, too!"

> (*They all laugh.* CHARLIE *joins in, if a bit weakly, and commences, aimlessly, to arrange glasses and bottles on the table.*)

JULIE

Must have been *some* party last night.

SYLVIA

(*Removing gloves and stole, and putting them down, with her purse*)

The greatest!

JOE

The most!
    (CHARLIE *rattles glasses together, nervously.*)

JULIE

What was it—an occasion of some kind?

SYLVIA

Indeed it was!

CHARLIE
    (*Hastily*)
Well—we better start looking for that earring, hadn't we?
    (*Stooping to look for the earring.*)

JULIE
    (*Demandingly, to* SYLVIA)
What kind of an occasion?

SYLVIA

A happy occasion.

JULIE

What do you mean—"a happy occasion?"

CHARLIE

Must be around here somewhere!

SYLVIA

Why, it was—what is this, Miss Gillis? A third degree?

JULIE

Well—I've got a right to know.
(*Glares at* CHARLIE.)

SYLVIA

What right?
(*Looks at* CHARLIE. CHARLIE *groans, ducks behind the bar.*)

JOE

Just a minute! I have the horrible feeling that I know what this idiot boy has done! (*To* JULIE) Miss Gillis, were you by any chance here last night—say between six and seven?

JULIE

Yes.

JOE

Where did you disappear to?

JULIE

I got sick. Charlie took me home. We went out to celebrate. We ordered silver fizzes. We didn't know there was egg white in them.

JOE

Celebrate what?

JULIE

Our engagement. Charlie proposed to me.
(SYLVIA *reacts.*)

JOE

I see. (CHARLIE's *hands appear above the bar. He follows them slowly into view. He looks miserable.* JOE *speaks to* JULIE) Well, my child, shortly after you were taken home with your lumps last night, Charlie had a whacking big party to announce his engagement—his engagement to Sylvia, that is—not to you. Maybe he's planning another party for your engagement later.

JULIE

Charlie—is that true!

CHARLIE
(*With great weariness*)
Yeah.

JULIE
(*Trembling, gasping with fury, she shouts*)
You knew it! You knew all the time there was egg white in a silver fizz! You did it just to get rid of me!

CHARLIE

Honest, I didn't. You can think anything you like of me, but that I swear I didn't do!

JULIE

You did, too! Of all the contemptible—I never want to— you are the worst—(*Out of control she rushes to* CHARLIE, *and starts to whack him over the head with her purse*) You terrible, terrible, terrible man!
(*She beats* CHARLIE *to the floor, out of sight, then runs weeping out the front door.*)

THE TENDER TRAP

CHARLIE

(*Rising from behind bar, after a moment*)
Why, that girl is nuts. She ought to be locked up—hitting people with pocketbooks! (*Finds a glass of whisky on the bar*) Who knows what's in a silver fizz? She thought it was a pretty name. (*Tosses off the drink*) Hitting people with pocketbooks! To think I might have married that nut! Boy! (*He lifts the glass again, remembers his manners, offers it to* SYLVIA) Sylvia?

SYLVIA

No.

CHARLIE

Well, here's to you. You're my kind of girl. You're all right.

SYLVIA

Gee, thanks.

CHARLIE

It's you and me, Sylvia—and a good thing, too. I'm a lot better off with you.

SYLVIA

There is some evidence to support that point of view.

CHARLIE

And, besides, I asked you first, didn't I?

SYLVIA

Yes, I believe you did.

CHARLIE

So everything turned out fine after all, didn't it?

SYLVIA

Dandy.

CHARLIE

Well—didn't it?

SYLVIA

Charlie, there are some girls who might not think this was the most romantic engagement on record. There are some girls who might even say our whole courtship left something to be desired. As a matter of fact, I am one of those girls. But, all in all, I agree with you. Everything turned out fine.

CHARLIE

Yes, sir—you're the girl for me, Sylvia.

SYLVIA

And you're the guy for me.

JOE

No!

SYLVIA

No—what?

JOE

No, Sylvia—it's all wrong. You can't throw yourself away on him!

CHARLIE

What do you mean—throw herself away? What am I—chopped liver or something?

JOE

That's not the point, Charlie. The point is—she doesn't love you.

SYLVIA

I certainly do.

CHARLIE

She certainly does!

JOE

Come on, Sylvia. Be honest with yourself. What did you say about him last night? "Eligible, attractive, employed, reasonably sane"—does that sound like a love letter?

SYLVIA

Joe, I don't know what you're doing—but cut it out.

CHARLIE

I know what you're doing—and I'm not going to let you. (*To* SYLVIA) Don't listen to him.

JOE

Sylvia—honey—there are worse things for a girl than not getting married.

159

SYLVIA

Name three!

CHARLIE

What right have you got to be talking like this?

JOE

Please, Charlie—I'm only thinking of Sylvia.

CHARLIE

The *hell* you are!

JOE

All right then—I'm not.

CHARLIE

Joe—make some sense, will you?

JOE

Sense? I stopped making sense the minute I laid eyes on this girl.

CHARLIE

Joe—you've *got* a wife!

JOE

(*To* SYLVIA)

And you knew it, because it happened to you, too. Now what should we do? Pretend it didn't?

SYLVIA

In a word—yes.

JOE

I can't—

CHARLIE

Joe—

JOE

I found what I thought I'd never find again—a girl—

CHARLIE

Joe—

JOE

A girl who's beautiful, and bright, and fun—

SYLVIA

I don't want to hear about it.
    (*The doorbell rings, persistently.*)

JOE

You've got to hear about it.

CHARLIE

Joe—have you lost your mind?

JOE

Answer the door!

CHARLIE

You can't do this—you just can't.

JOE

Answer the door! Sylvia, you've got to listen to me—
(CHARLIE *goes to the door, opens it, and* EARL *dashes in, followed by a weeping* JULIE.)

EARL

(*Backing* CHARLIE *down a couple of steps*)
What do you do to her up here? Every time I come around she's running out the door crying. What are you, a sex maniac, or something?

JOE

(*Indicating envelope under* EARL's *arm*)
Is that the report?

EARL

(*To* CHARLIE)
Don't think you're getting away with this, mister!

JOE

Excuse me. Is this the report?

EARL

(*Absently*)
Yeah. (JOE *snatches the envelope from under* EARL's *arm. He removes some typewritten pages from the envelope.* EARL *says to* CHARLIE) I never liked you from the beginning. And I'm through working for you. So you can write your company to find themselves another boy.

JOE

(*In great excitement*)

Earl—do I read this right?

EARL

Yeah.

JOE

Eighty-three percent effective?

EARL

Yeah. (*To* CHARLIE) No, by George, I'll write the company myself! I'll tell them what kind of a man they've got representing them in New York!

JOE

Charlie, did you ever hear of such a test in your life! Eighty-three percent effective.

CHARLIE

Hmm? Oh, yeah—yeah—great—(*He starts toward* JULIE) Julie—

EARL

(*Meets* CHARLIE, *blocking his way*)

You keep away from her!

CHARLIE

I just want to tell her I'm sorry—

EARL

Sorry! A lot of good that does! Why, back where I come from—

CHARLIE

Why don't you go back there!

EARL

Now, listen here—I don't care how tough you think you are—

JOE

Quiet! Quiet! Sylvia—I've got to talk to you. Let's get out of here.

SYLVIA

Not me, kid. I just established a beachhead.
(*Sits.*)

JULIE
(*Weeping*)

I want to go home.

EARL

You bet you do. And that's just where I'm going to take you!

JOE

No! Wait! Julie—stay. Earl—you go!

EARL

No, sir—I'm not leaving without Julie.

JOE

Then would you just step out on the terrace for a few minutes?

EARL

No, sir!

JOE

Julie, please ask him to go. This is important.

JULIE

Not to me, it isn't.

JOE

Believe me, it is. Now, ask him—please.

JULIE

Go on, Earl. I really would like to hear what he has to say that's so important.

EARL

Okay—but I'll be watching!
(JOE *hustles* EARL *onto the terrace, and closes the door.*)

JULIE

All right—now what's so important?

JOE

Just this. You love this guy—
(*Points to* CHARLIE.)

JULIE

I most certainly do not!

JOE

(*To* CHARLIE, *indicating* JULIE)
And you love her! Well? . . .

EARL

(*Bursting in from terrace*)
Hey! There's a dead fish out here!

JOE

Earl—will you please get the hell out of here?

EARL

I will not!

JOE

Earl—

EARL

I'm not going to stay on any terrace with any dead fish!

SYLVIA

Charlie—would you care to comment on Joe's statement about you and Miss Gillis?

CHARLIE

Well, I—but the whole thing is just—I mean—what can
I—?

SYLVIA

This has been, all in all, a memorable day. If my luck
holds out, I should get hit with a truck on the way home.

JOE

Sylvia, let's get out of here. We've got so much to talk
about. The pill is a great success.

EARL

Success?

JOE

Don't you see—everything's possible now.

EARL

What do you mean—success? That pill is no good!

JOE

Eighty-three percent effective is no good?

EARL

The first test, sure. What about the other one?

JOE

What other one?

EARL

The second test. (*Looks at papers* JOE *holds*) It must still be in the envelope. (*Extracts another sheet from envelope*) Oh, yeah—here it is.

JOE

What's this?

CHARLIE

Zero!

EARL

That's right. Zero.

JOE

But I don't get it. Eighty-three percent effective on the first test, and zero on the second?

EARL

Remember what you told me? Those two ingredients locked in a death grip? Boy, you're right. They murder each other.

JOE

I don't—

EARL

It's the old story. Unstable compound. Three days out of the vat, and it turns into something entirely different which is no good whatsoever for the common cold.

(CHARLIE *turns away.*)

THE TENDER TRAP

JOE

But there must be some way to make it work!

EARL

Sure. The minute somebody sneezes, stick him in a plane, fly him to Indianapolis, rush him to the Van Husen Company, and shove his head in the vat. It shouldn't cost more than a thousand dollars to cure a cold.

JOE

He was right. The old man was right again. He'll be rubbing my nose in this for years.

CHARLIE

Yeah. And Ethel's going to have a couple of things to say, too.

JOE

Oh, no. The one time I don't have to worry about Ethel is when I'm in *big* trouble.

SYLVIA

That's right, Joe. It's a property of wives, sticking with their men when they're in *big* trouble. And there's a couple of other properties that go right along with it—like wall-to-wall carpeting and a house full of kids, all of them with good straight teeth. It's what you call a package deal.

JOE

And you want the same package, huh?

SYLVIA

Sure. What did you think? Moonbeams? Candlelight suppers? Cloud number seven? Joe—you know what you've got? You've got the married man's dream. You want a girl. That's what you all want—a girl. And that's what you never get—because the only way to have girls is not to marry them. After that they become wives—which is something entirely different.

JULIE

And a good thing, too. Somebody's got to take care of you.

JOE

Do they?

SYLVIA

Well—look what happens when you get away from home.

JOE

(*After a pause*)

On behalf of the visiting firemen from Indiana—I thank you.

(*Bows to the girls.*)

SYLVIA

So long—fireman. (*Goes to* JOE, *kisses him*) Where the hell were you twelve years ago?

(*Goes to door.*)

CHARLIE

Sylvia—what can I say? . . .

SYLVIA

(*At the door*)

Say "Good luck"—because there'll be no more second best for me. I'm going to find me an honest-to-God guy who's looking for an honest-to-God girl. Somewhere in this great city, there must be one!

(*Goes.* JOE *picks up picture of his wife and children.*)

JOE

Yup! (JOE *starts for bedroom with picture.* EARL *stares at it.* To EARL) The woman who takes care of me.

(*Goes into bedroom.*)

JULIE

Charlie—

EARL

Now, Julie. Can we get out of here now?

JULIE

In a minute. Charlie, can you give me any explanation at all for your conduct last night?

CHARLIE

No.

EARL

Come on, Julie.

JULIE

But surely you must have had some reason.

EARL

(*Tries to pull* JULIE *toward door*)
Come on, Julie. Don't get mixed up with this guy again.

JULIE

Earl, will you mind your own business?

EARL

What is it, Julie? Do you want to stay? Do you enjoy this kind of treatment?

JULIE

I am merely trying—

EARL

You are merely staying because you like it!

JULIE

Charlie, I know that basically you are not a wicked person.

EARL

Wicked! This guy could give Jack the Ripper cards and spades! Good-bye!
(*He slams out the door. A silent moment.*)

JULIE

Well—I'll be going.

CHARLIE

Uh-huh.
(JULIE *starts for door.* CHARLIE *seems to pay her no attention. At the door, she pauses.*)

172

JULIE

Aren't you going to try to stop me?

CHARLIE

No, ma'am! Not me!

JULIE

But don't you love me?

CHARLIE

Yes, I love you.

JULIE

Well, then—why don't you try to stop me?

CHARLIE

Well, to be perfectly frank—I'm scared of you.

JULIE

All right—I'll admit I got overexcited. But what do you expect from a girl in love?

CHARLIE

I don't know what to expect. If love makes people this crazy, what can marriage be like? Brother!
(*Shudders.*)

JULIE

(*Soothingly*)

Now, Charlie, marriage is nothing to be afraid of—
(CHARLIE *makes a doubtful noise. The bedroom door opens,*

and JOE *appears behind* JULIE *and* CHARLIE. *He starts for the front door, carrying his suitcase.* JULIE *continues)* What is it but love and companionship and tenderness and devotion and—

JOE
(*As he goes up the steps*)
And dancing lessons and fencing lessons and dramatic lessons—(*Turns at the door*) Say—I've got a great idea. Why don't you two get married?

CHARLIE
Married?
(JULIE *gives* CHARLIE *a melting look.*)

JOE
Can you think of a better idea?

CHARLIE
Doesn't seem to be anything else to do, does there?

JOE
Never is. Never was. (*Puts down suitcase*) So long, Charlie.

JOE
(*Shakes* CHARLIE's *hand*)
Thanks for the hospitality. Kiss the bride?

CHARLIE
Be my guest.
(JULIE *offers her lips to be kissed.* JOE *rejects them.*)

JOE

Uh-uh!
> (JOE *pushes up her sleeve, and kisses the inside of her elbow. Then he turns, slaps* CHARLIE *affectionately in the belly, and exits.*)

JULIE

He's really awfully nice—but very mixed up.

CHARLIE

Who isn't?

JULIE

I'm not. Charlie—I love you.

CHARLIE

> (*Nodding his head with some sadness*)

Yes.

JULIE

I do, you know.

CHARLIE

Well, I love you, too. That's why we're getting married—

JULIE

When should we do it, Charlie?

CHARLIE

Oh, the sooner the better. Let's get it over with.

175

JULIE

We could get the license tomorrow.

CHARLIE

Okay. I'll meet you down at the license bureau at precisely ten hundred hours.

JULIE
(*A trace of severity*)

You'll *what!*

CHARLIE

I'll pick you up at your house and take you down to the license bureau.

JULIE

That's better.
(*He sits beside her. They exchange a loving kiss.*)

CHARLIE
(*Cuddling her in his arms*)

Now let me see if I've got it all straight. We live in New York for two years, and then we have a baby. At Doctors Hospital. And then we move to Scarsdale. And we buy a nice little split-level. And we cover it with wall-to-wall carpeting—

JULIE
(*Sitting up*)

No!

CHARLIE
(*Sits up*)

No?

JULIE

I don't like wall-to-wall carpeting.

CHARLIE

You don't? (JULIE *shakes her head. Making a grab for her,*
CHARLIE *says*) Come here!
    (*They embrace.*)

CURTAIN